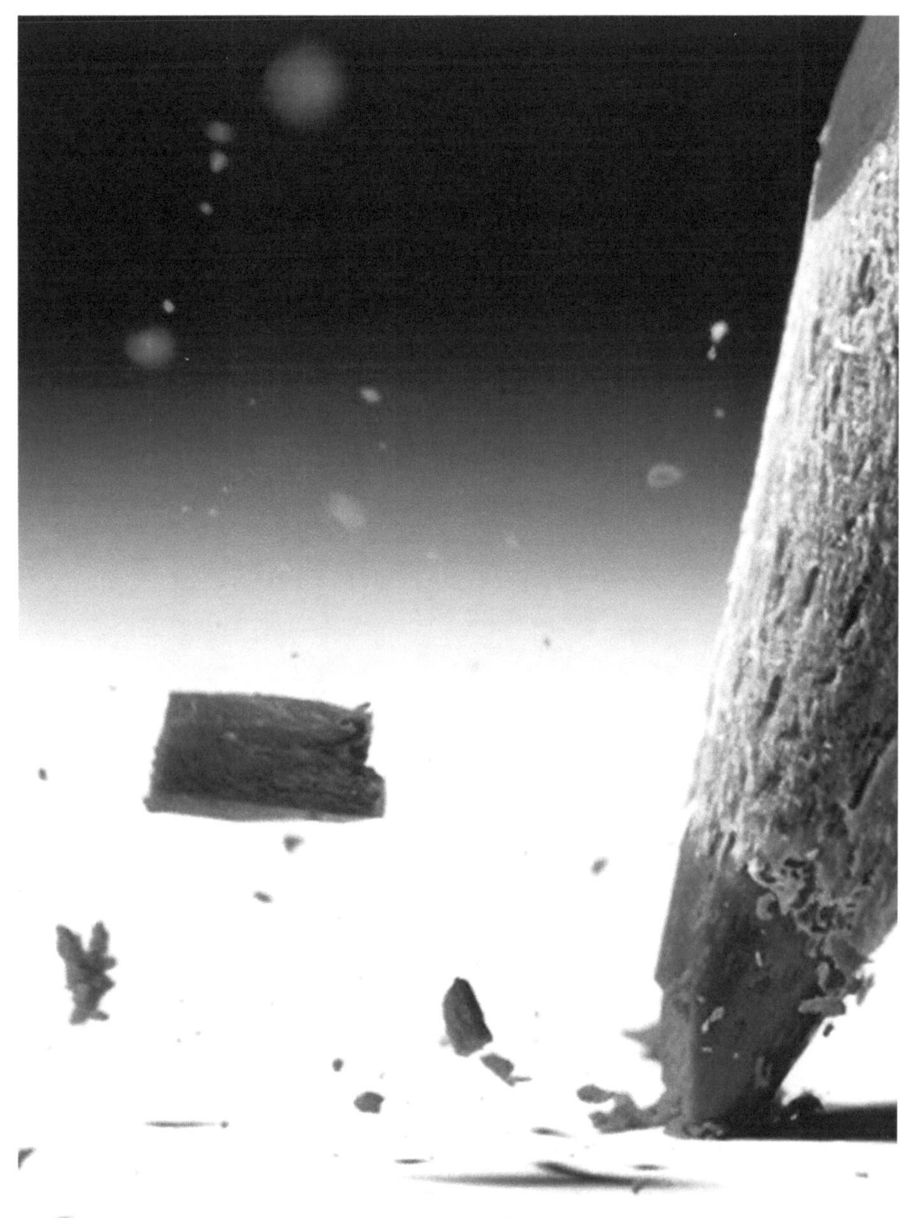

"This book is my breath and dreams so don't waste this book"

"Don't read success stories,
you will only get a message.
Read failure stories, you will
get some ideas to get success"

Dr. A.P.J Abdulkalam

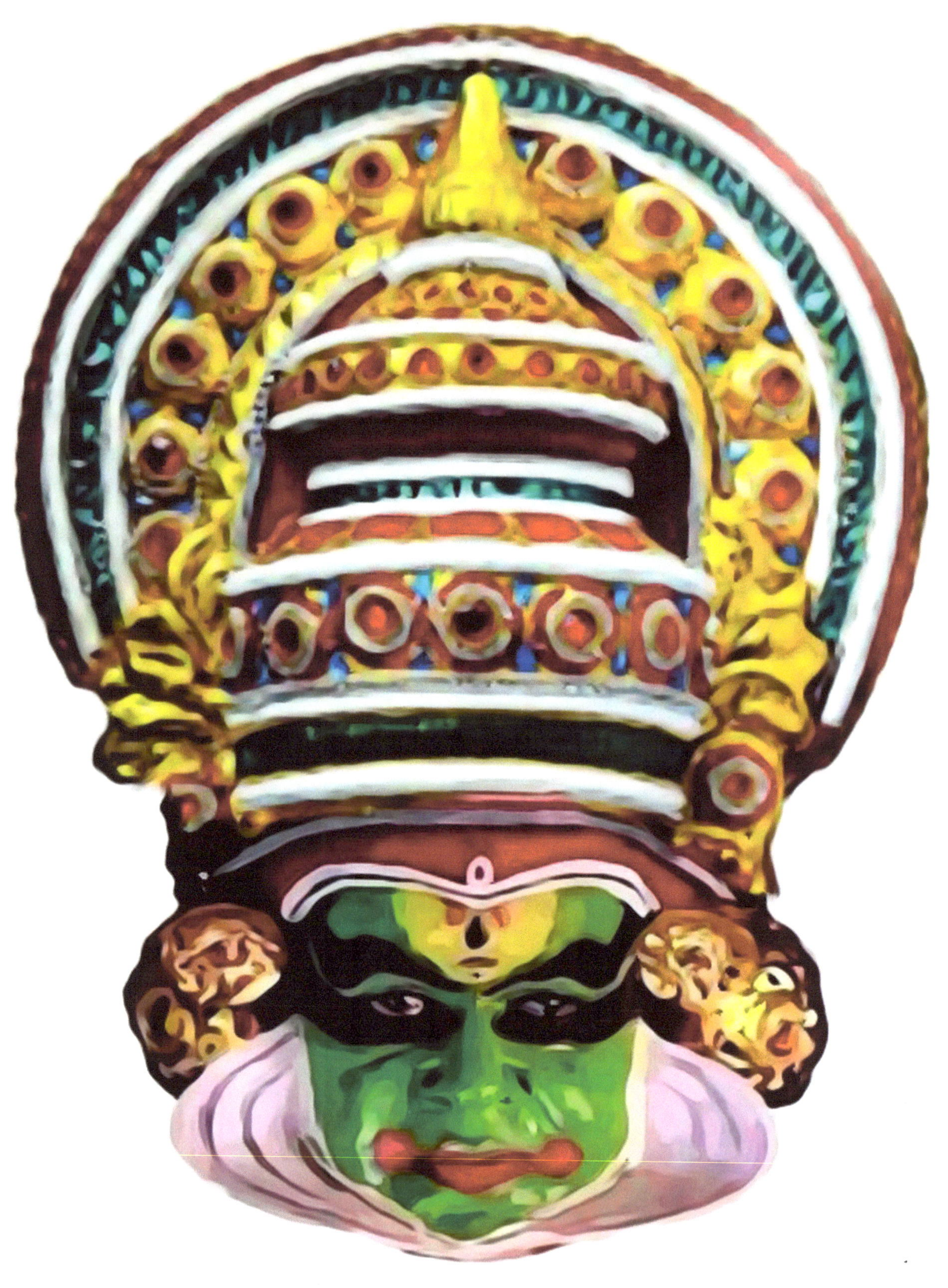

kannan

ഹൃദയത്തിന്റെ കൈയൊപ്പ്

മോഹൻലാൽ

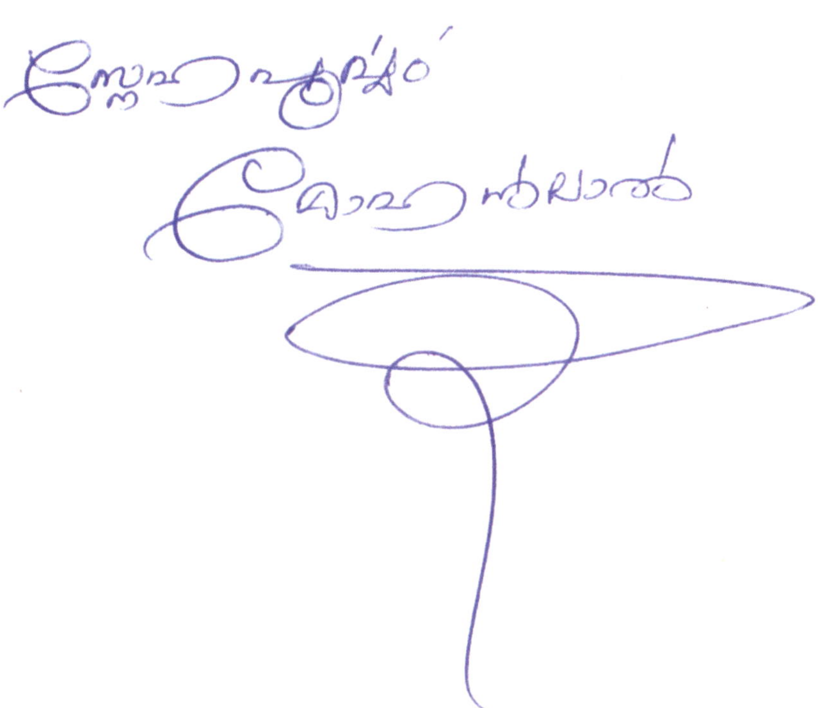

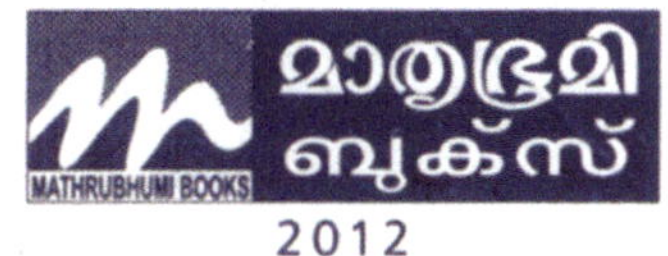

2012

This book has helped me a lot to overcome my loneliness. I experienced a lot of depression when I stopped drawing, and that stage is still a struggle for me. I managed to escape from this stage by reading, and thus I found the book. It is a valuable resource for me, as it has become my enduring best friend. It is no longer an external source. The words in this book are both powerful and provide me with mental support. Now, I feel that I am not alone in this world. I appreciate you granting me the gift of a best friend. I am thankful for God's autobiography with heartfelt thanks.

Thank You Lenaa.

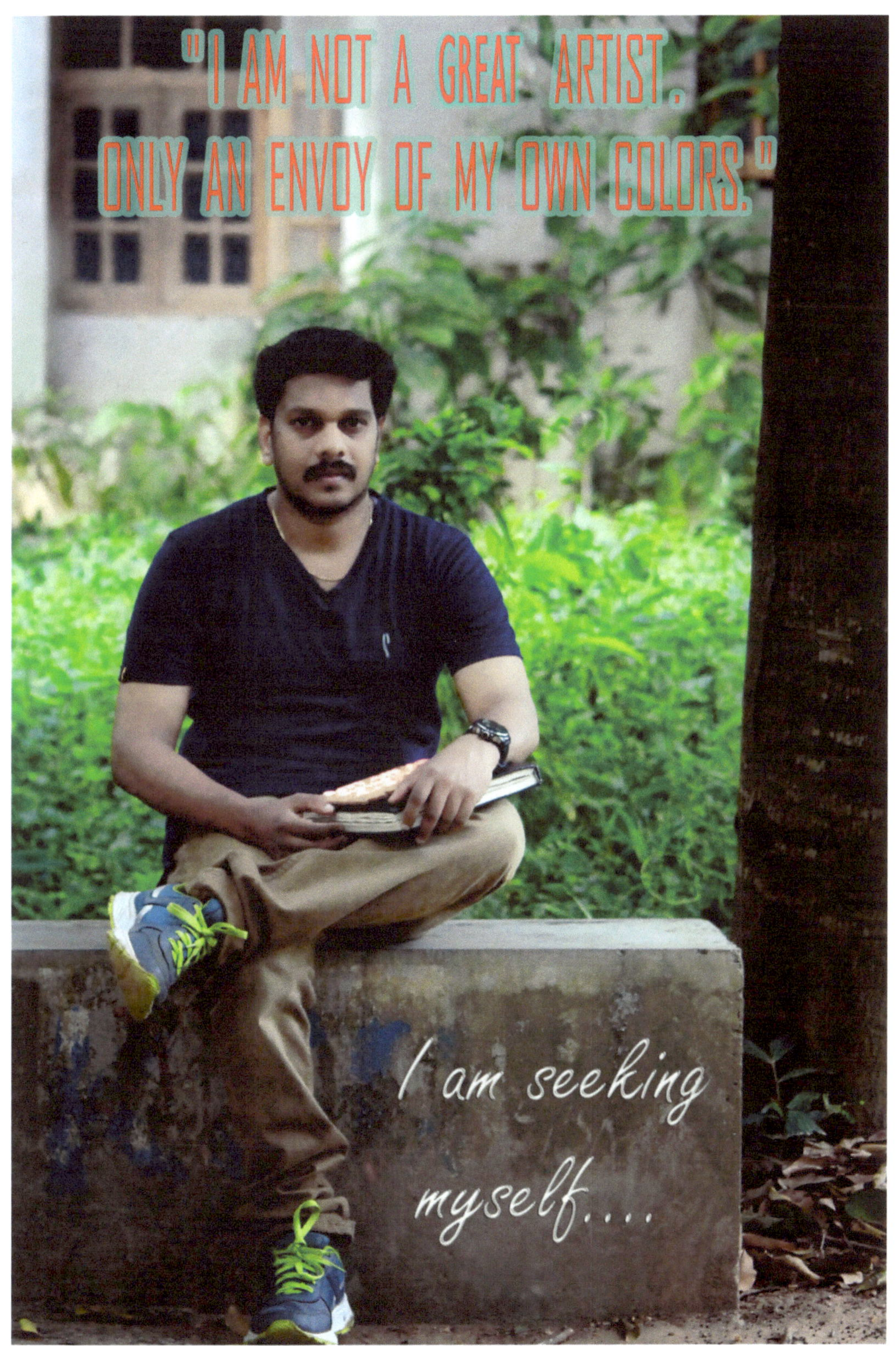
"I AM NOT A GREAT ARTIST,
ONLY AN ENVOY OF MY OWN COLORS."
I am seeking
myself....

The awareness of one's own inner strength makes one modest.

Kannan joined Sree Sankara College as a student of Zoology Department in 2010.

His first year went uneventful. Nobody knew the budding artist. However, soon Kannan began to associate himself with the creative circle of Renaissance, a Multi disciplinary Center for research, Extension and Learning, and during his second year in the campus, he conducted the first exhibition of his paintings.

His paintings have a rarity that is mystifying to a lover of painting. He mixes realism with his personal symbols, and drifts off from photographic realism.

He is a soulful painter who meditates on the kernel for a long time before executing it. Only when stirred to the act, does he take the brush. The emotional tide slowly gets transformed into a painting.

Though Kannan is tossed up in the upheavals of personal struggles, he keeps the colours of passion as embers within.

Kannan, on the personal side, does not change colours according to situations. He is genuine and loving.

I wish him all the best.

Dr Sujeesh C. K.
Coordinator, Renaissance
Sree Sankara College, Kalady

03-12-2019
www.facebook.renaissancesankara

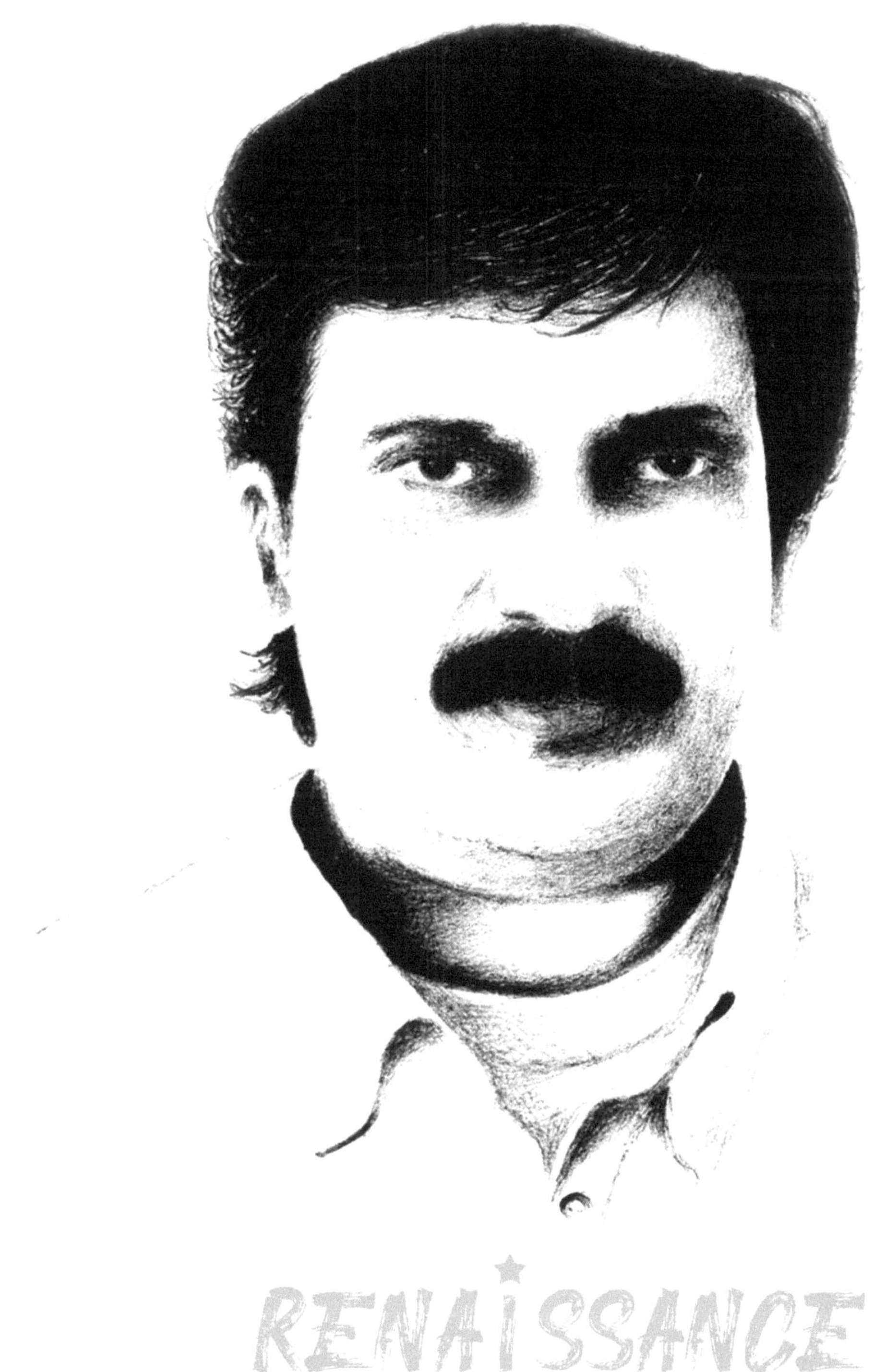

RENAISSANCE
kannan

I am introducing to a lot of you who like drawings and their silent ideas this series of explorations, which haven't reached anywhere, through some creations that I have experienced and lived through. I haven't been schooled in painting and have never been trained by a good master !. I still hold the wish to learn painting. Hence, experts in this art, do pardon me ! As I share my ideas with you, I am also hoping to receive comments from you in return. From this, I will be receiving an energy that I haven't gotten before. Just like the saying goes, "Boost is the secret of my energy," this is part of my efforts to open a closed door.

Art... A person who expresses himself or herself through a medium.
"My responsibility as an artist is to convey beauty to the people and to find the wonderful side of things."

You know the energy that comes through while creating with your own hands. The last time I had to think and draw... I found myself there. It was heart rending and that motivated me to write about it.

Nevertheless, at present, I forget about myself. That is my condition now.

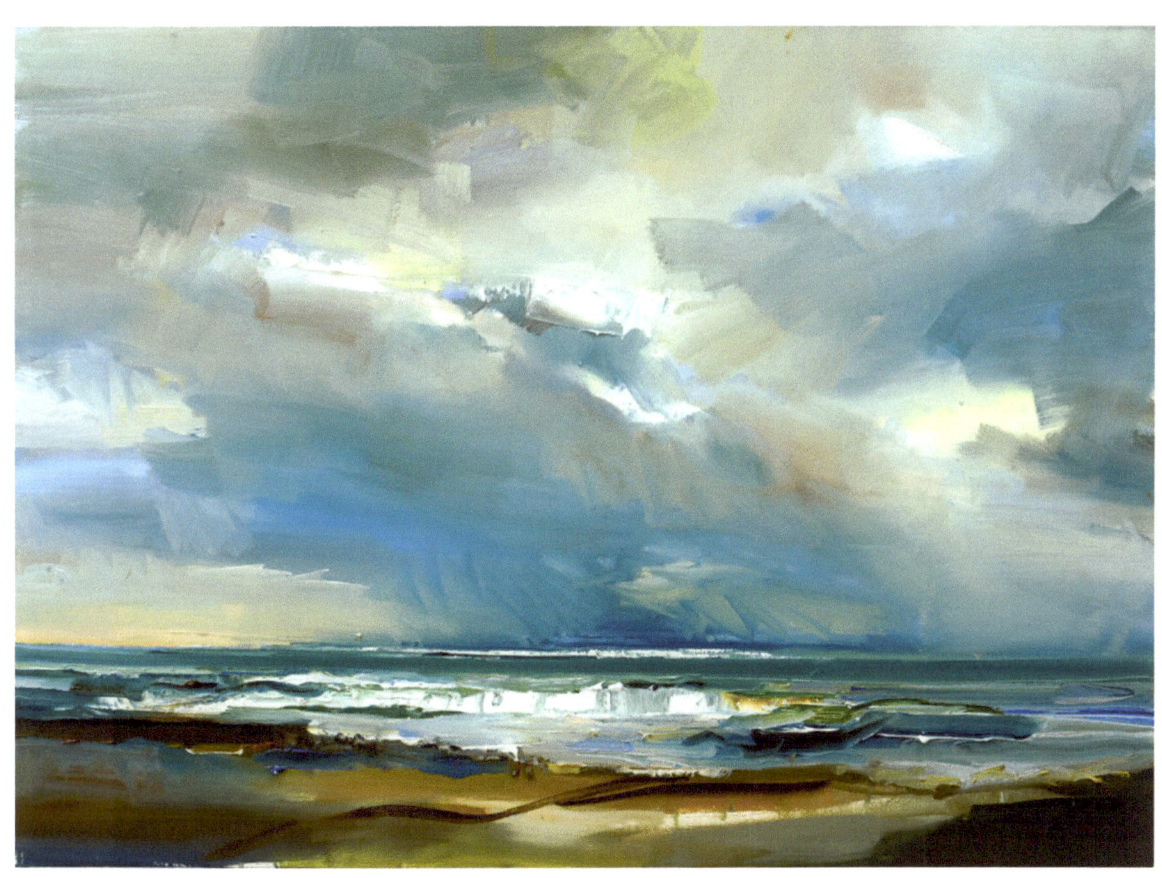

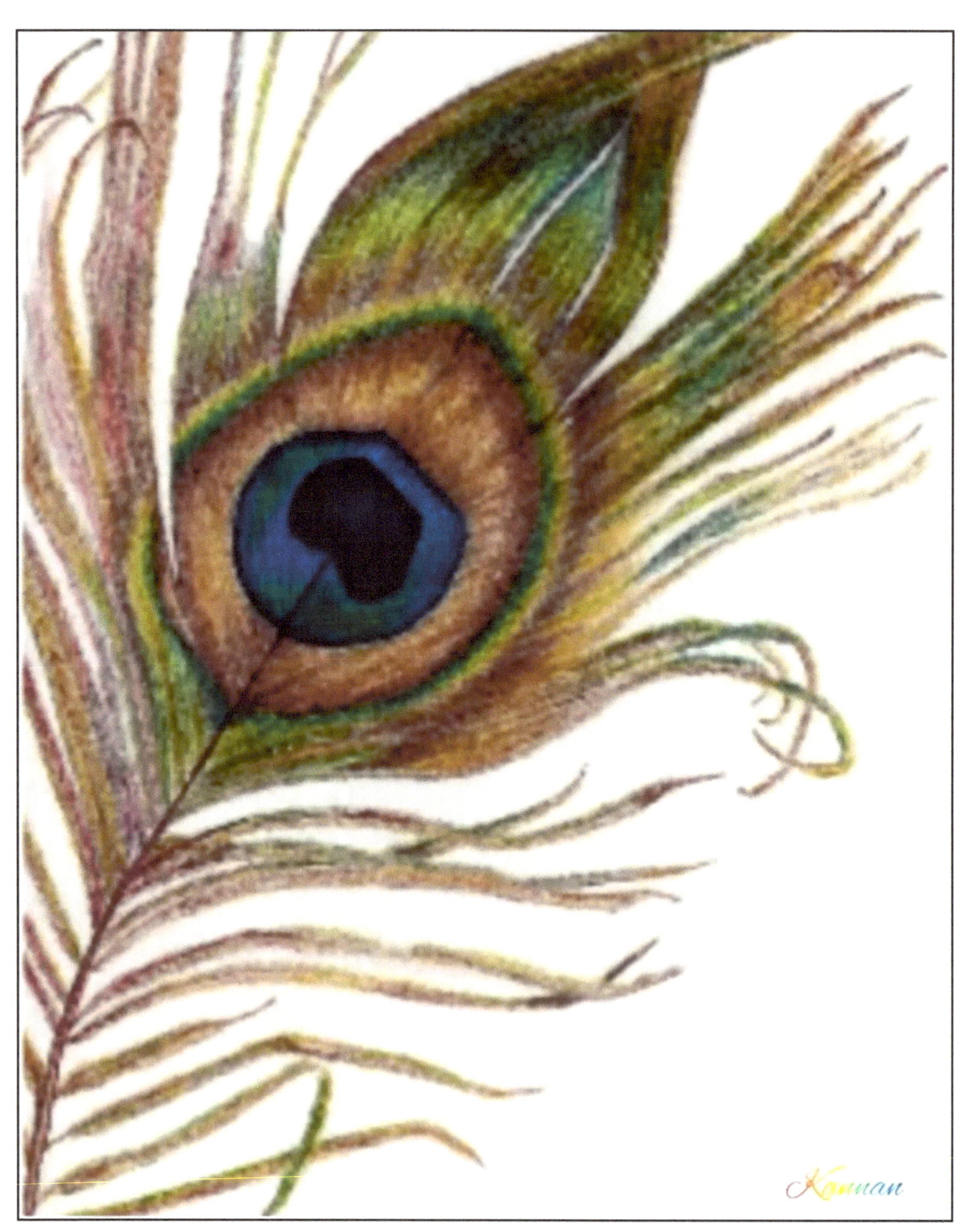

CONTENTS

Through the Life of Colors:
A Creation!

People have asked why apple has been included when they have seen the picture after some changes were made to the ideas. This is a symbol of sweet romance. The words of Blaise Pascal is apt when he says, "Imagination Decides Everything." For the birth of a good picture, imagination is inevitable. A characteristic of oil painting from my experience is that no matter how much has already been painted, there is a feeling to paint again and again. The mind will transcend into a new world. I get the colours I like from there. It is this confluence of colours that gives life to each and every painting!

Within the painting, I should be able to feel eyes and a mind full of life. This feeling is immense for a painter. It is from the creation of eyes that I get the beats of life. The thing that I garnered from this painting is a colour combination that took a permanent place in my memories. People have told me about the 'eyes full of life' when they talk to me after they have laid their eyes on this painting. This, I consider, as an appreciation for the creation of eyes.

The presence of apple next to this character is an important one. It must be a love story full of sweetness that she is reading. The apple symbolizes that. How can one share an experience of love with those who cannot understand true love ? How can someone who has never tasted alcohol experience the buzz from it ? True love is like that only. I am not promoting alcohol consumption here... But, not to get technical... According to chemistry, alcohol is a solution...

To be a one woman man... i.e., one preferring or seeking romantic involvement with one woman only, it is here that true love exists.

Painting is not something that can be completed in an instant. We have to mould our hearts so that we can delve deep into that creation. Every creation happens after we achieve that. It takes time for a tree to grow a sweet fruit on it. We have to give the tree time to make the fruit a sweet one.

The tree has to give time so that it can grow a sweet fruit out of it. So is the time required for a painting. The mind can't rest until beauty is obtained. If you want to weave beauty in a way you like, then you can definitely change your mind about the image.

"Get your heart and hand free, and touch the beauty; my hand will move in any direction of beauty."

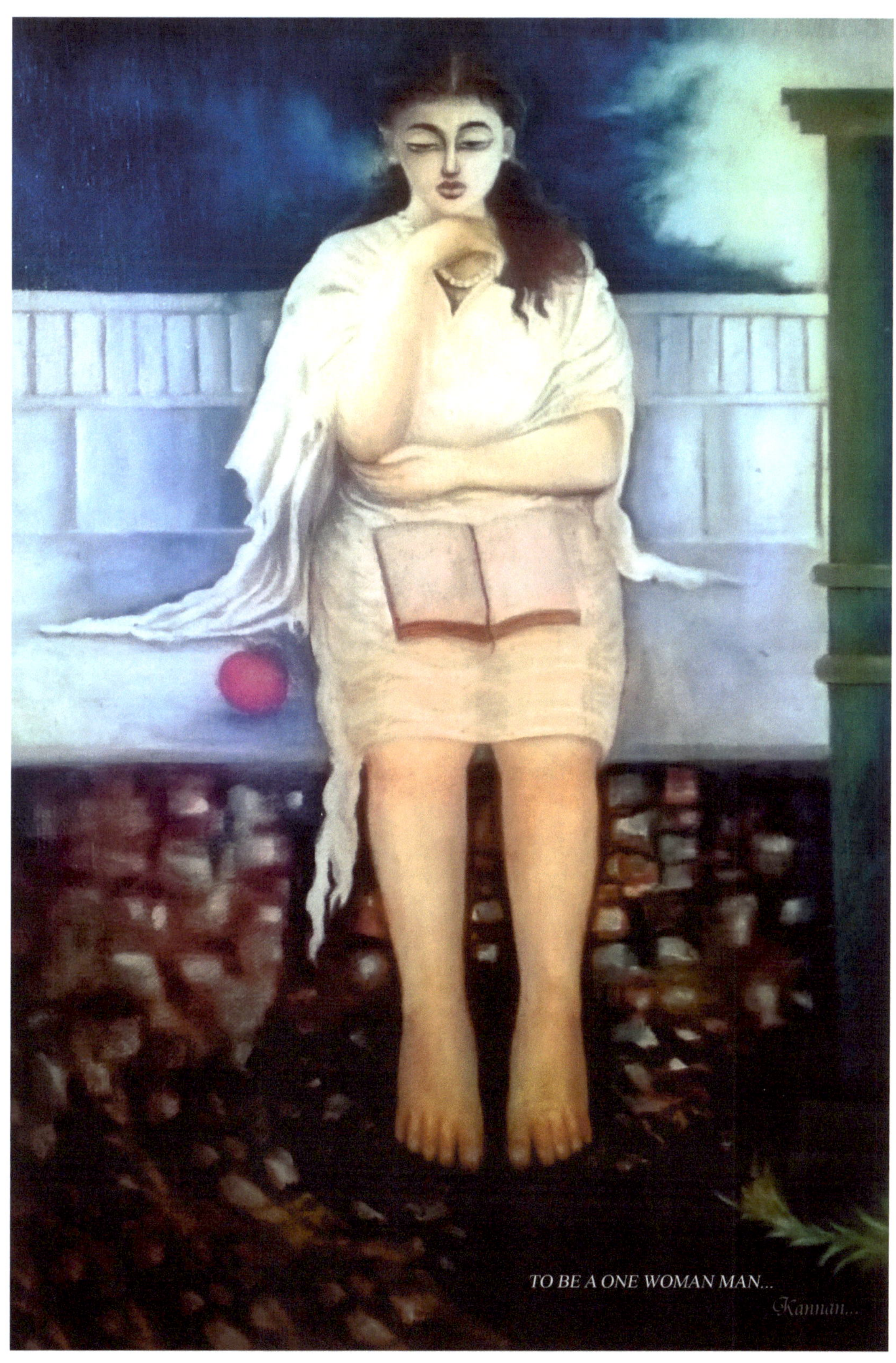

TO BE A ONE WOMAN MAN...
Kannan...

The God
We Don't See

God is in different forms. For the blind, God takes the form of sound. But, for us, we have different faces for our gods: Hindu, Islam, Christian... Why does society persist with communalism in the name of God even now? I do not understand their mind... I am not interested in knowing it. But there is something that they do not understand.

When 'sound' becomes God and dives into the ears, what is the basis of the communalism created in society in the name of God by the ones who have the ability to see with their eyes?

The God created by the communal mobs is at a permanent loss in front of the blind, who understand the God as 'sound'.

Why do you think that God exists or does not exist?

"A child you do not know; he is suddenly faced with death. If you felt sad, you wept, or you cried for a kid that you did not know much about... Your loving heart is God."

"You are searching for God without realizing the God within you."

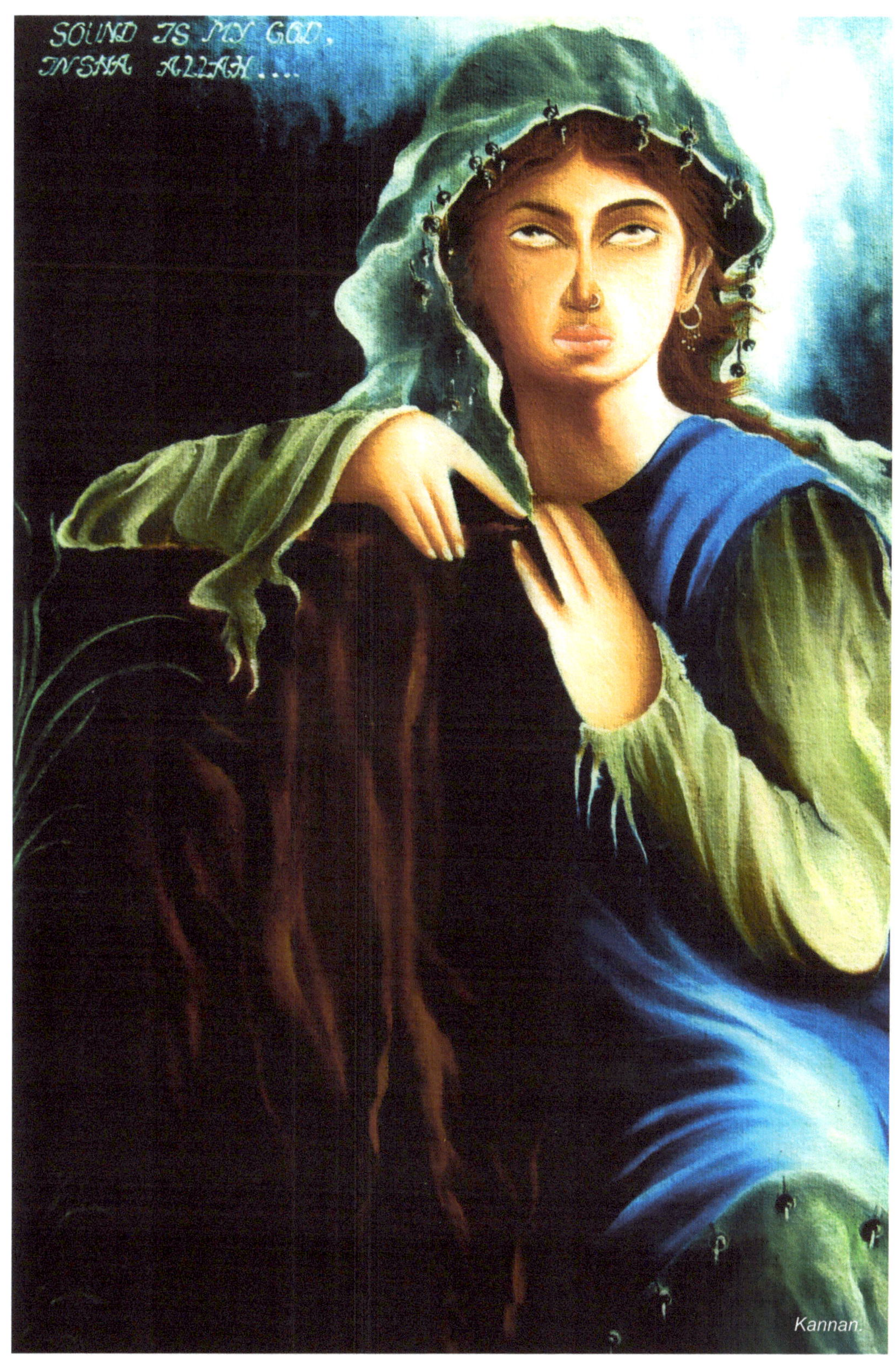
SOUND IS MY GOD.
INSHA ALLAH....
Kannan.

**God Who is
Only Mine**

I still have a pain in my mind

that I did not draw my deity.

"I have no words to express

my feelings for you.

My heart still beats only

because of you.

You are my heart."

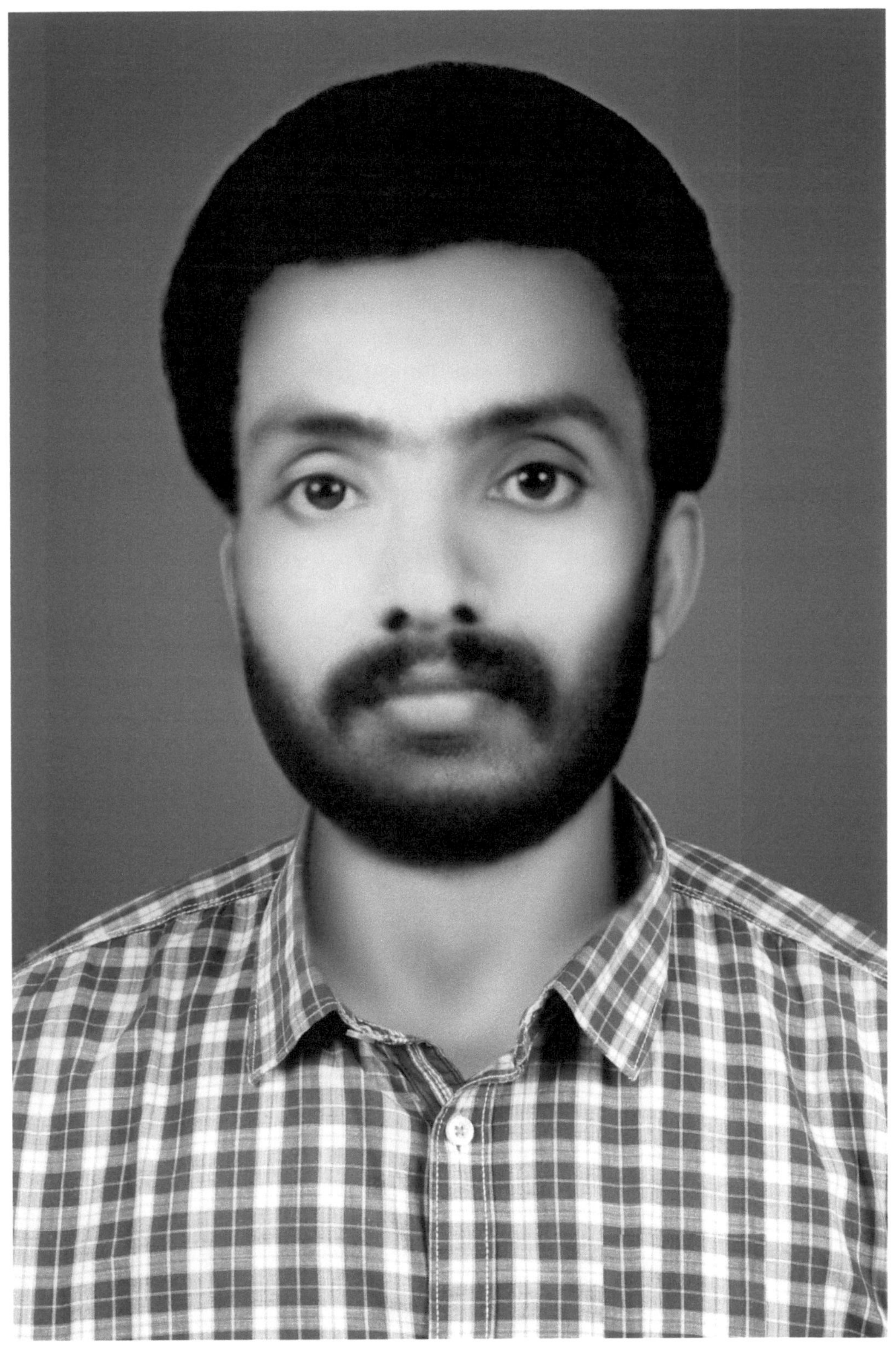

A Journey Through
the Mind of a Child

Traveling gives me knowledge, visions, and happiness. However, follows the journal from my journey through the mind of a child...

A child's observation is on the bubbles; the child observes them, which float around him and above him. If you look closely, you can see seven colours twinkling inside the bubbles—the colours that always sparkle. They change from one to the other throughout. This brings joy to him. He enjoys the bubbles without knowing the life of the bubbles. He enjoys the visual beauty of the bubbles that appeared to him fighting the darkness around him. Even though the life of the bubbles is short, it is wonderful to see the emotions that take birth in him.

These emotions and appreciations are lost when one grows from a child into an adult. Do we adults have the same feelings when we see bubbles in front of our eyes ? Therein lies the difference between the mind of a child and that of an adult. This is similar to certain situations and people who leave our lives without us realizing they are gone: people with plenty of goodness in their hearts, the helpless, loners, and ones with no political power. The needs of a common man are important in this context. There is a common man inside you too. You have to realise that.

"I am no one special; just a common man with common thoughts. I have led a common life. That's my lifestyle, and that's what I try to bring to my characters."

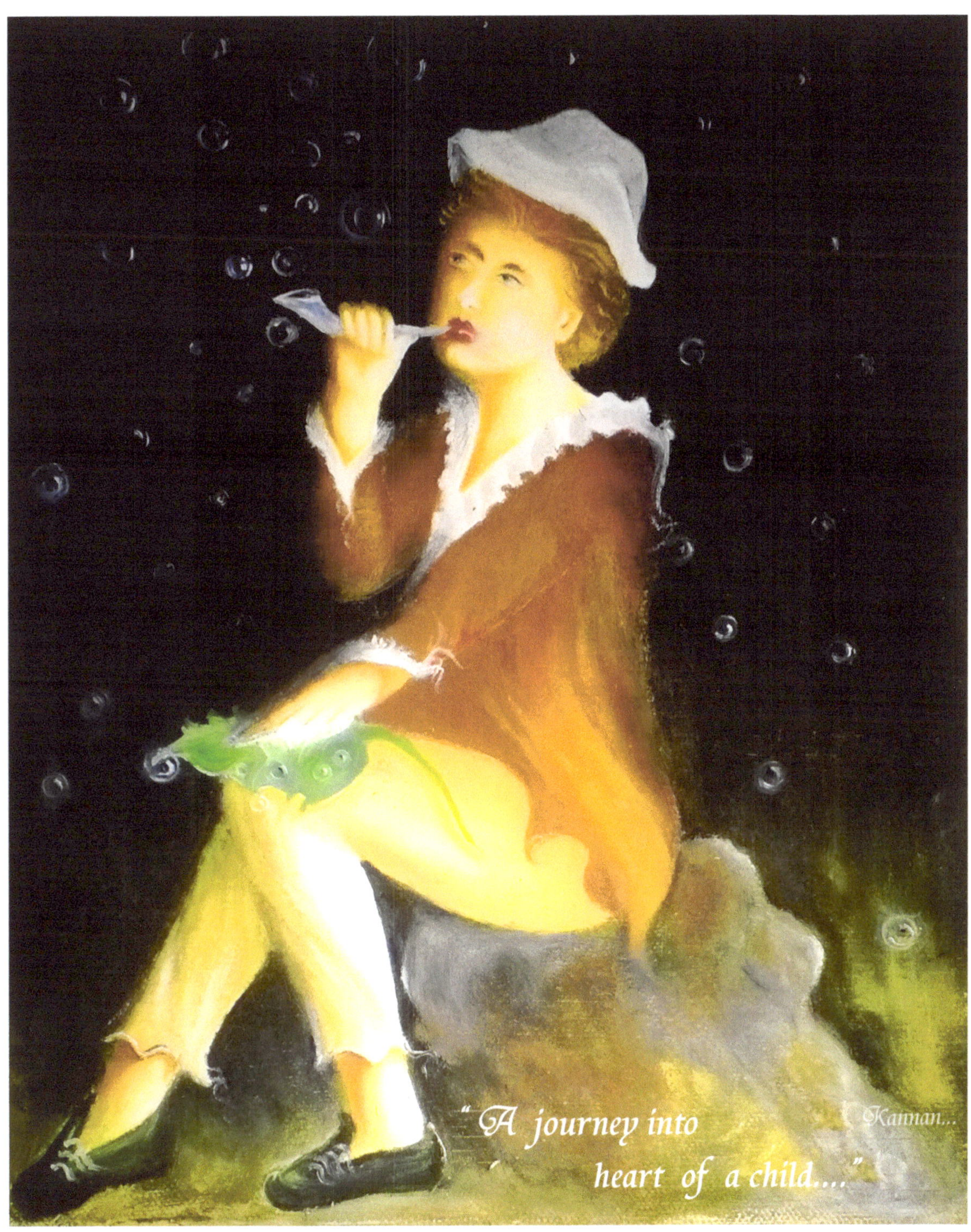
" A journey into
heart of a child...."
Kannan...

Moon Love

Sun is alone too, but it still shines. Universe without the sun is swallowed by the darkness. However, the luminance of the moon is cold and evokes a feeling of chillness. The moon is a companion to our dreams. As the sun sets, the next day is born with new hopes. The moon's position in dreams is a great one. I have included the moon in many of my paintings where the scope of imagination is greater. I am a selenophile when it comes to painting the moon. It happens without our knowledge.

"Live by the Sun,
Love by the Moon."
If you truly love nature, you will find... beauty everywhere.

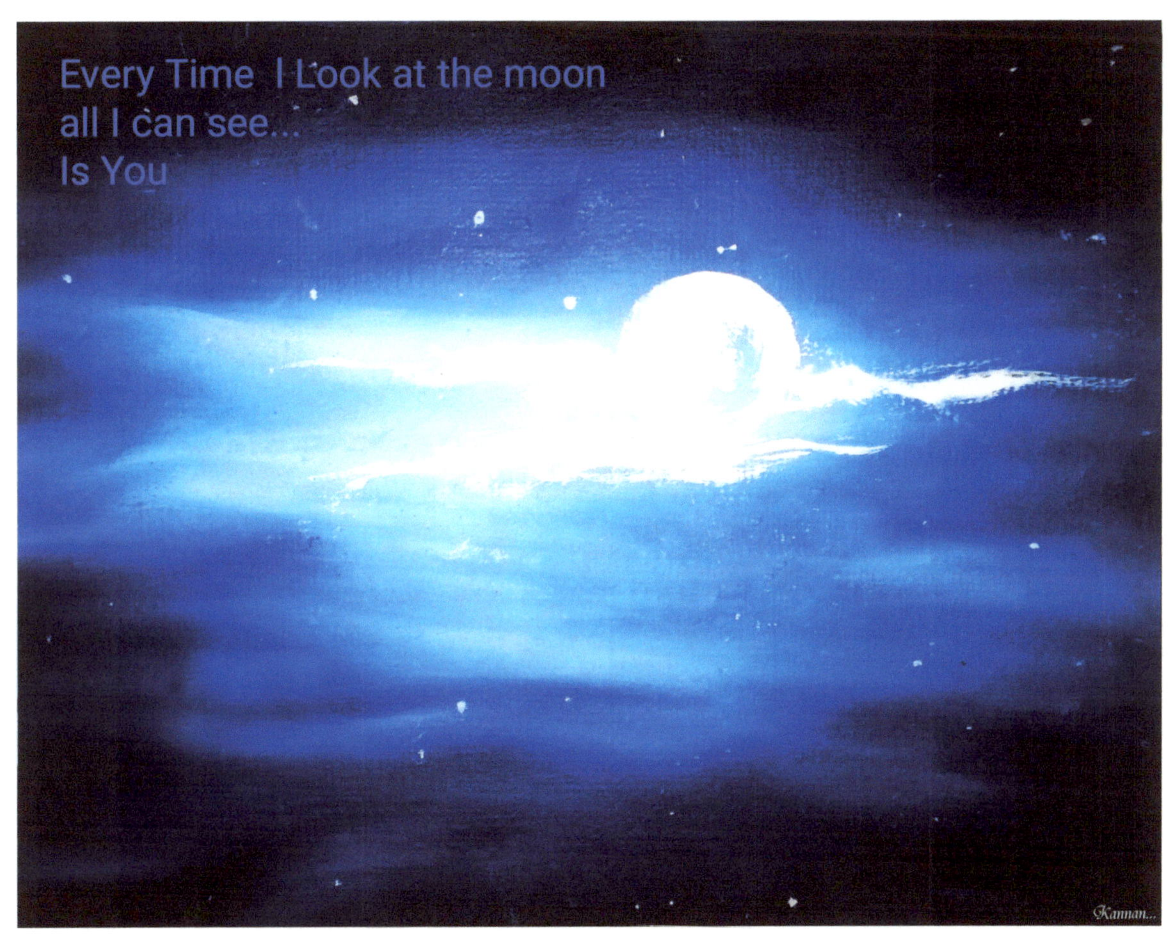

Every Time I Look at the moon
all I can see...
Is You
Kannan...

Some Tear Drops
That No One Sees

Some tear drops that no one sees... Those who have experienced it at least once will understand the condition of not being able to express their grief openly to anyone. There are also people like this in the world we live in. We do not see it, or they hesitate to show it to this world. The situation of those who live calmly outside but with tears inside is depicted in this painting.

This painting is among the ones that hurt me when I was doing the watercolors on it. I have experienced and learned all their grief-ridden conditions from their eyes. While writing the captions, my fingers trembled unknowingly.

"What you hide in your heart
is read in your eyes."
This is my art. It comes from deep within me.

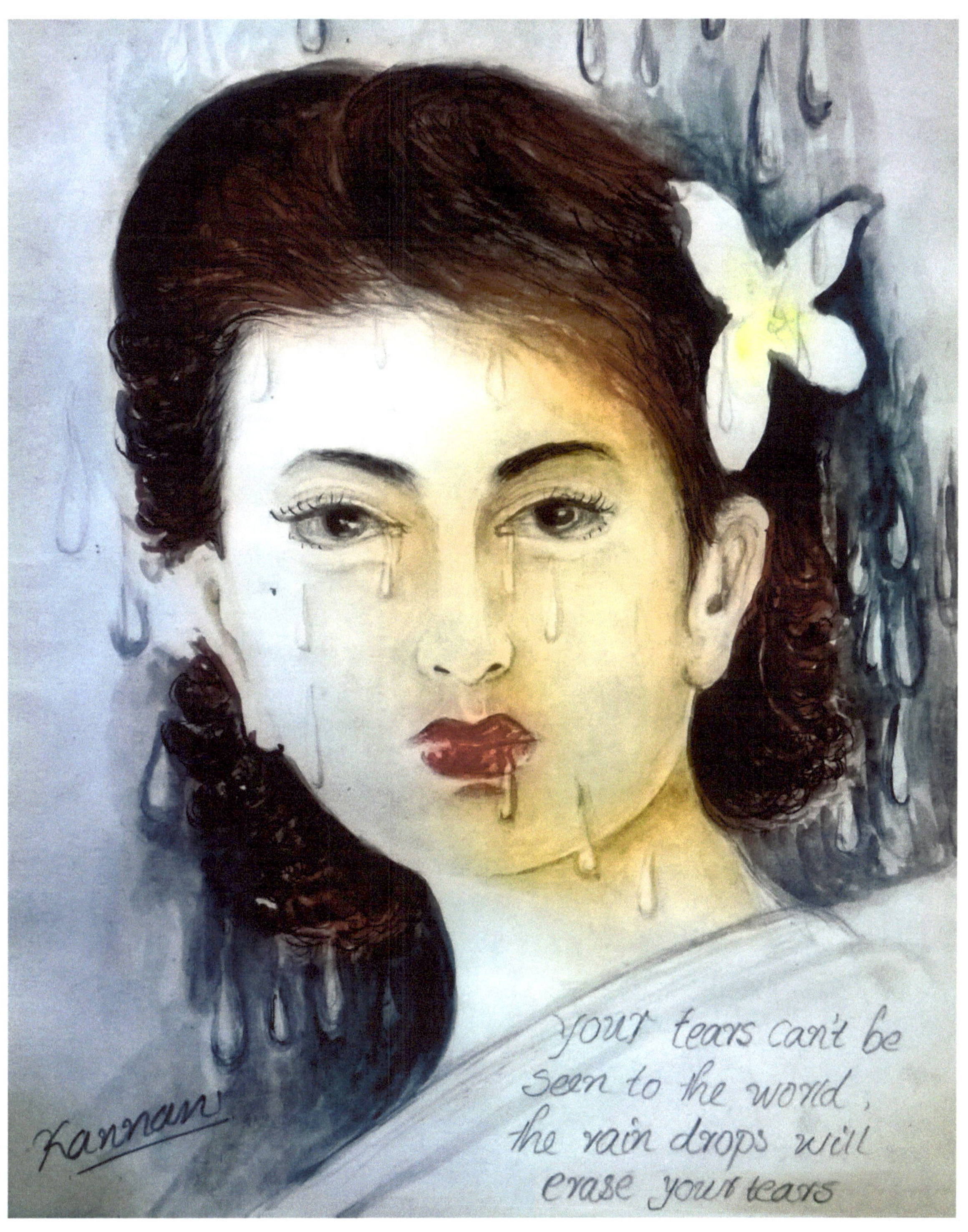
Kannan
your tears can't be
seen to the world,
the rain drops will
erase your tears

Which Word is most Important?
'Yes' or 'No'?

Which Word is most Important? 'Yes' or 'No'?
Why 'No' is the most important word... you will ever say half of the troubles of this life can be traced to saying 'Yes' too quickly and saying 'No' soon enough.

I have enjoyed life a lot more by saying 'Yes' than by saying 'No'.

The significance of 'Yes' here is one that is deserved. But we have to give due importance to 'No'. 'No' is a complete sentence, and so often we forget that saying 'No' can be the ultimate self-care. When should we give importance to the word 'No'? It should be emphasized when a second person or the first person speaks it.

Touching, teasing, or depriving someone of their freedom without their consent is wrong. Even if it is a woman who sells her body for a living, if she says "No" it is still "No". We should be able to accept those words.

They don't wish to live after suffering torture. I have given the form of a snake for torture. I am comparing the snake here to a stern, terrifying, subjugating being. But they are not depicted as the reincarnation of Shiva.

"We should not let this happen in front of our eyes while we're all alive!"
"The aim of Art is to represent not the outward appearance of things but inward significance."

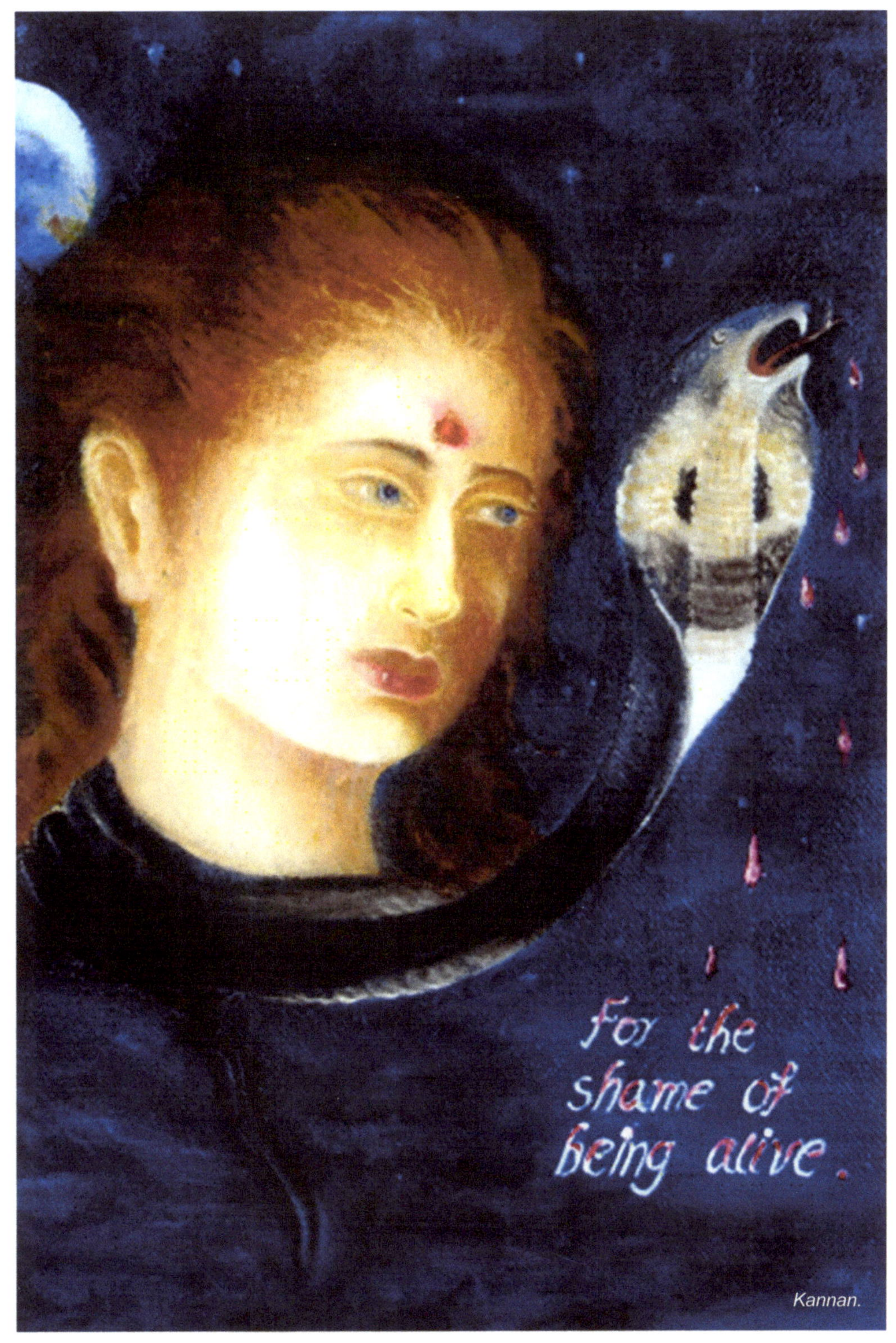

Kannan.

Moments of Life
that Conch Gives

I get a special feeling from every drop of water that falls from the conch. Conch was a favorite of my grandfather. He used to tell me how it was very valuable for him. Even when his visions began to fall on his eyes as darkness, he would ask for my paintings when I finished them. The smile that bloomed on his face surprised me. Because how does he see those creations when his eyes are failing him ? I still don't know about it.

What is special about the conch is that it has a life within. Even when that life has ceased to exist, it gives a sound experience that is full of life through its shell. When you place the conch close to your ear, it brings you the life of the sea.

For me, this book is like the shell of a conch. No matter where I am, your comments will give me life from this book.

"The only time I feel alive is when I am painting."

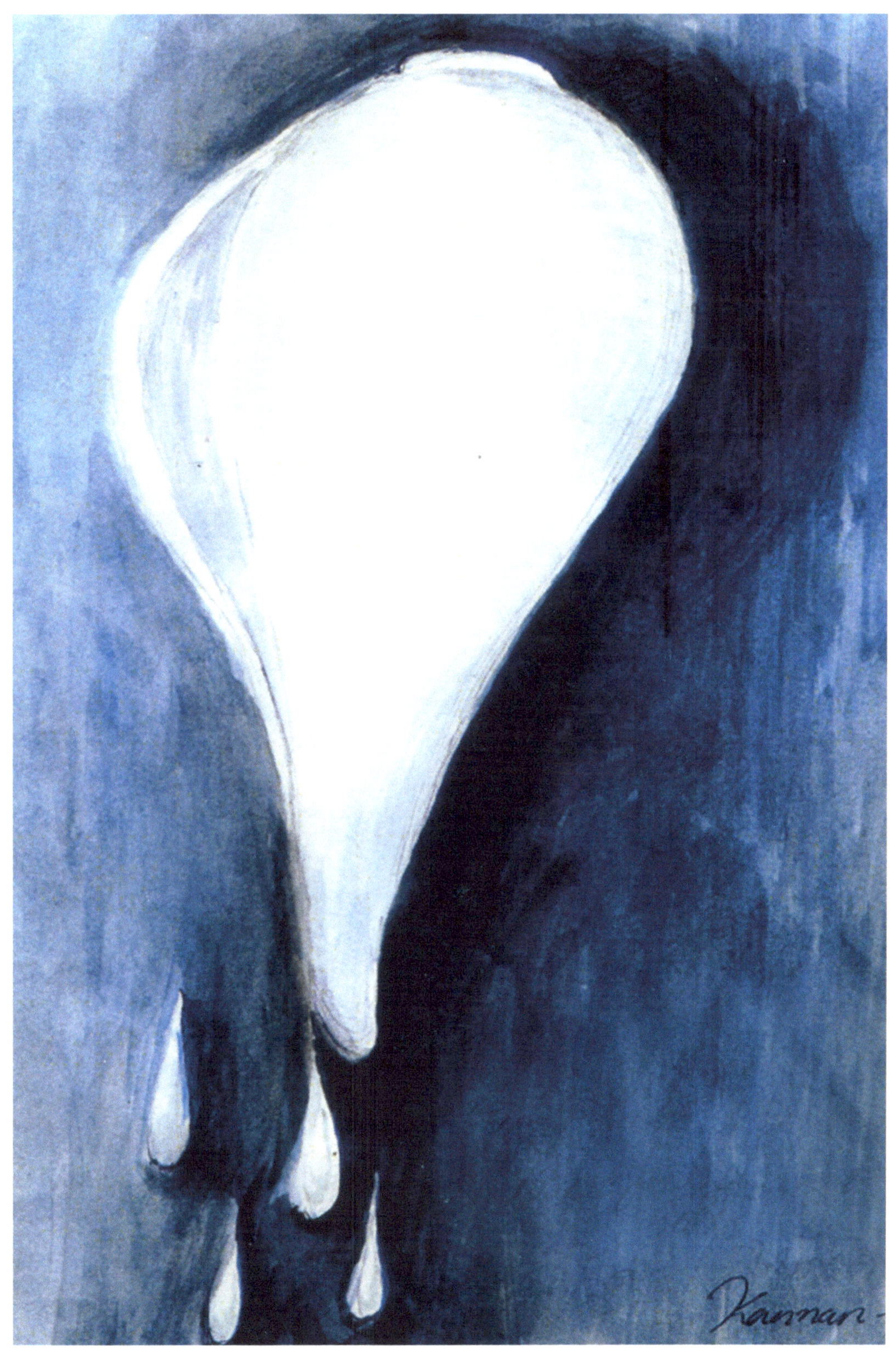

Kannan

My Love

Love is not completely defined; it is difficult to define. Sometimes the heart sees what is invisible to the eyes.

Here we are talking about the intense passion of love. The intensity of love is always reflected in the eyes. I don't know what the perfection of the same is. But it takes us to another world. That is the truth!

> "you can close your eyes to
> the things you do not want to see,
> but you cannot close your heart to
> the things you do not want to feel!"
> Johnny Depp

In the creation of this painting, I experienced the condition that takes over when the passionate love in the eyes descends deep into the heart. The reflection from the sun-drenched sands will look sparkling when we look from afar. I have noticed it often. The glitter in the grains of sand is due to the energy it receives from the sun. True love creates a similar energy between two people. If they can feel like this, then it is the same feeling I experience from this creation.

When idols are made, eyes are created at the very end of their creation. And the 'Mizhiturakal' (opening eyes) is the most auspicious part of sculpture. Similarly, a painter draws the eyes as the final act of creation. But I create the eyes first, because the eyes are luminance... Sight is the ability... That is what is lost... The grief over the same is indescribable.

"For the cares of deep love, what is the reply of the eyes? Is it silence...?So please don't kill that deep silence. It always lives in your eyes." Art speaks, where words Are unable to explain.

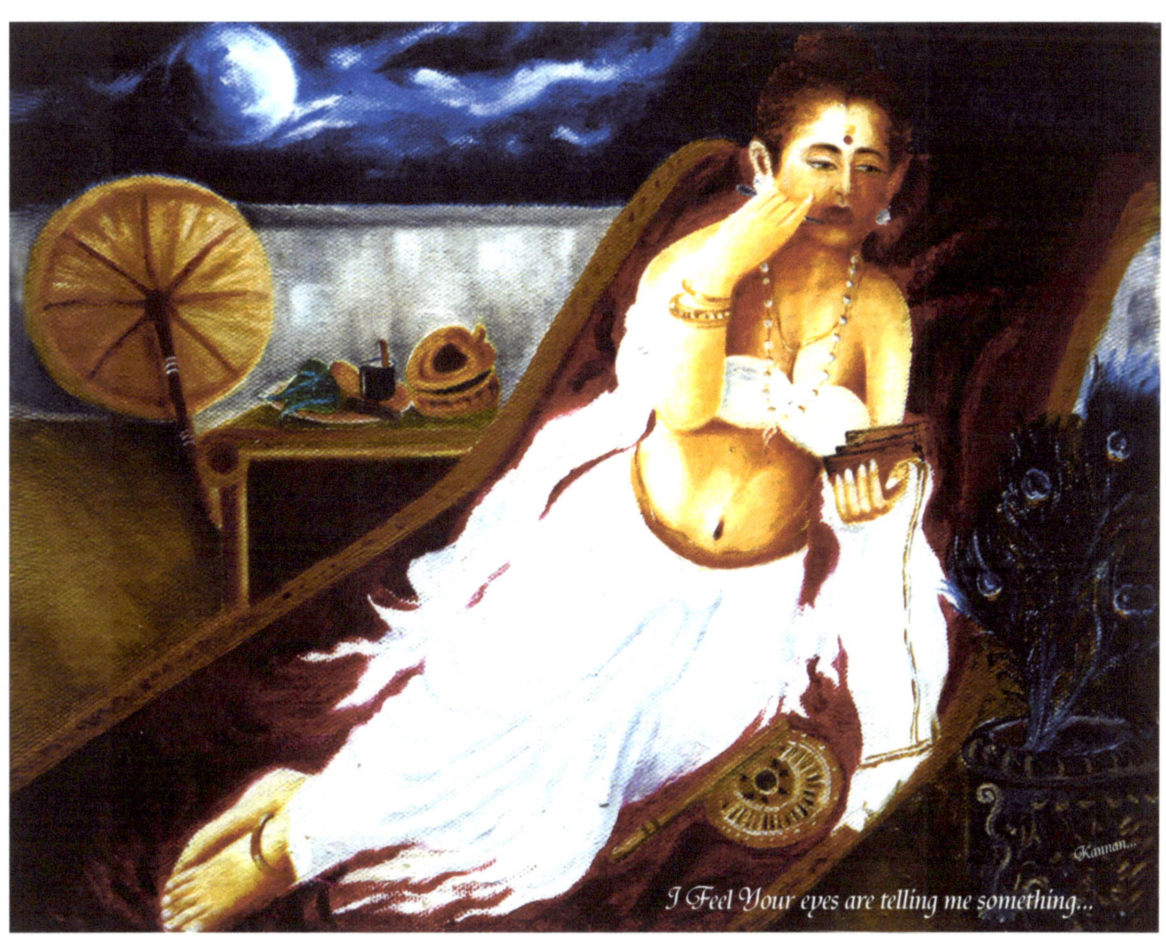

I Feel Your eyes are telling me something...
Kannan...

The Complete Actor Lalettan

It was a dream to draw a picture of Lalettan and gift it to him. Pencil drawing, oil painting—I drew them both. I don't know which one he likes more. It was at a time when I was trying to get to show him one of them that I learned Lalettan was coming somewhere near here. But there was a huge crowd that day. I have only really seen the beating of the police on TV. But that was the day I experienced it. Amongst the crowd was me and the drawing. I was also the one who stood at the front when it was even more crowded. His arrival created a great commotion. It was the body that took the beating by the police lathi. It was also in the mind that the pain stayed without healing. I stood there without wasting a single beat, protecting the drawing from any damage. It was a moment of pain and tears.

A few days later, I read in the newspaper that he was visiting Sree Sankaracharya University of Sanskrit, Kalady. At that time, my friend was the chairman of the college union. The matter was presented to him. There was no pain from the lathi there. After a while, Lalettan arrived. I don't know whether it was because I saw him in person or because I touched him, but no words came out. He has bright eyes that attract anyone. He saw the painting for himself on the stage and asked them to announce it. Laletan asked for oil painting first. But I didn't want to part with it. Please don't ask for this Laletta. I wanted to keep it with me forever. He was silent for a moment. He then smiled and said slowly, "Give me the pencil drawing. You should place it in my car."

There is a room in Lalettan's house just for painting. Wherever he went, he would bring a painting with him there. My pencil drawing is there. According to me, he is indeed a complete actor. I did not sleep that night. It had to be he himself who should have touched those oil paintings. My intention was to paint Lalettan from the movie 'Rajashilpi'. But I ended up drawing a new Lalettan. I value the touch of his heart more than a few trophies and certificates.

I have two more favorite actors: Ameer Khan and Pierce Brosnan. movies of Aamir Khan are entirely different. Aamir Khan is presenting different characters. All are good films. That is his talent. Satyamevajayate is a very good TV show that reaches out to the common people.

Pierce Brosnan...... The best actor in the world who showed the acting moments hidden in his eyes and eyebrows. His action scenes are particularly fluid. Pierce Brosnan is the true 007 James Bond. Amir Khan and Pierce Brosnan are also two actors who I wanted to draw.

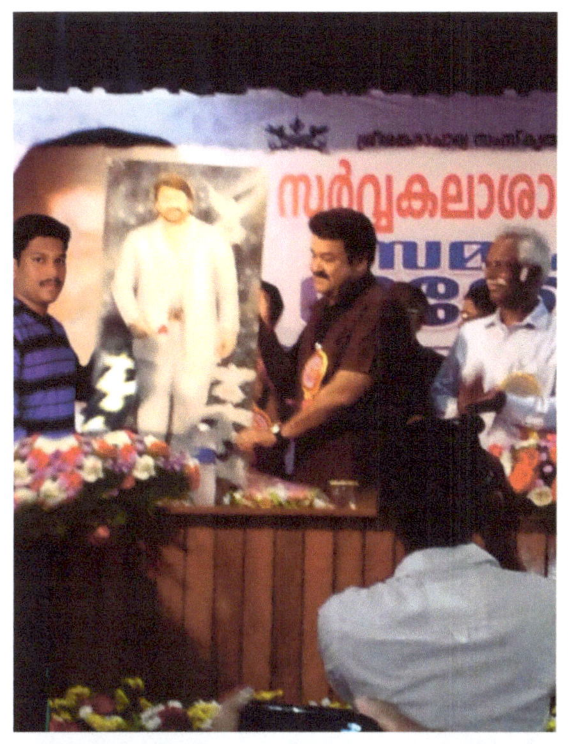
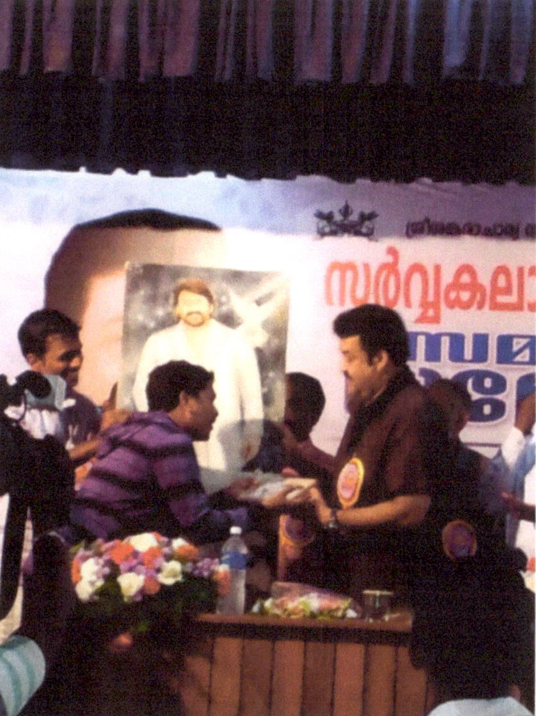
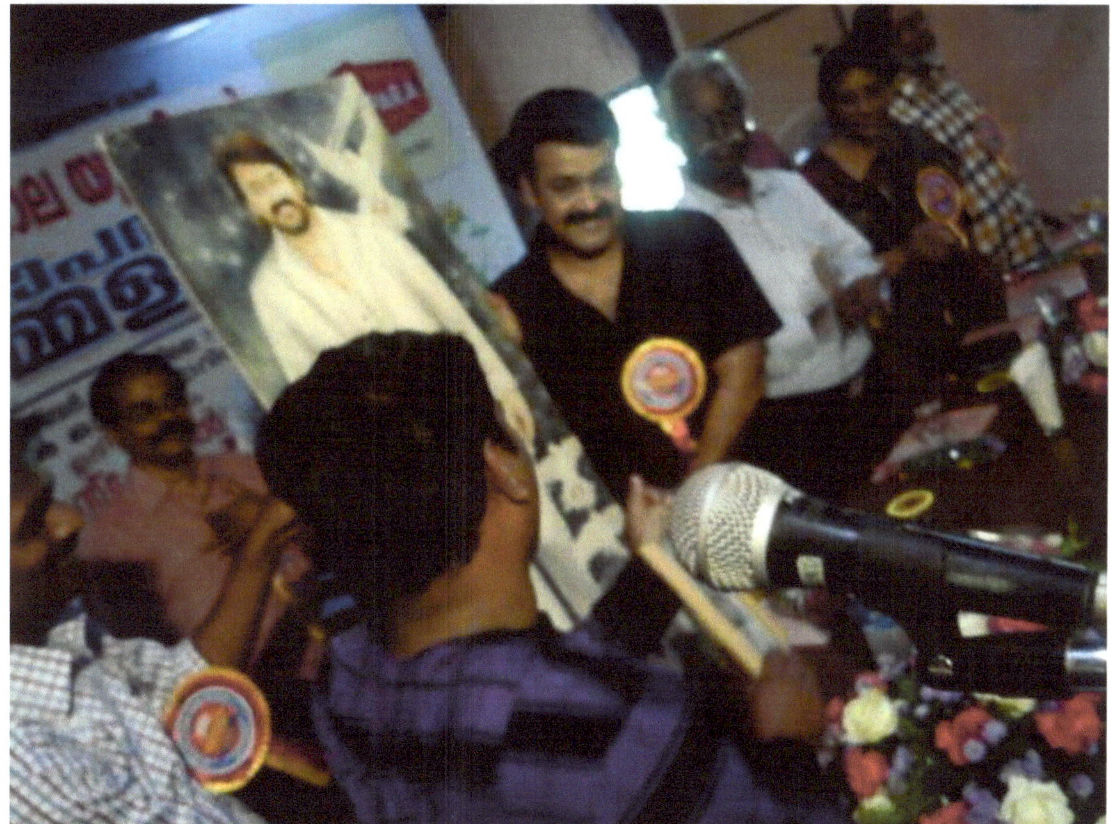

Best Actor

After a long time, we got a character with a good heart. An unforgettable personality. He gave life to the character of 'Joseph'. He was able to bring a distinctive character to life by portraying a face full of mysteriousness. Even after the release of the film, the acting personality you showed... It cannot be forgotten.

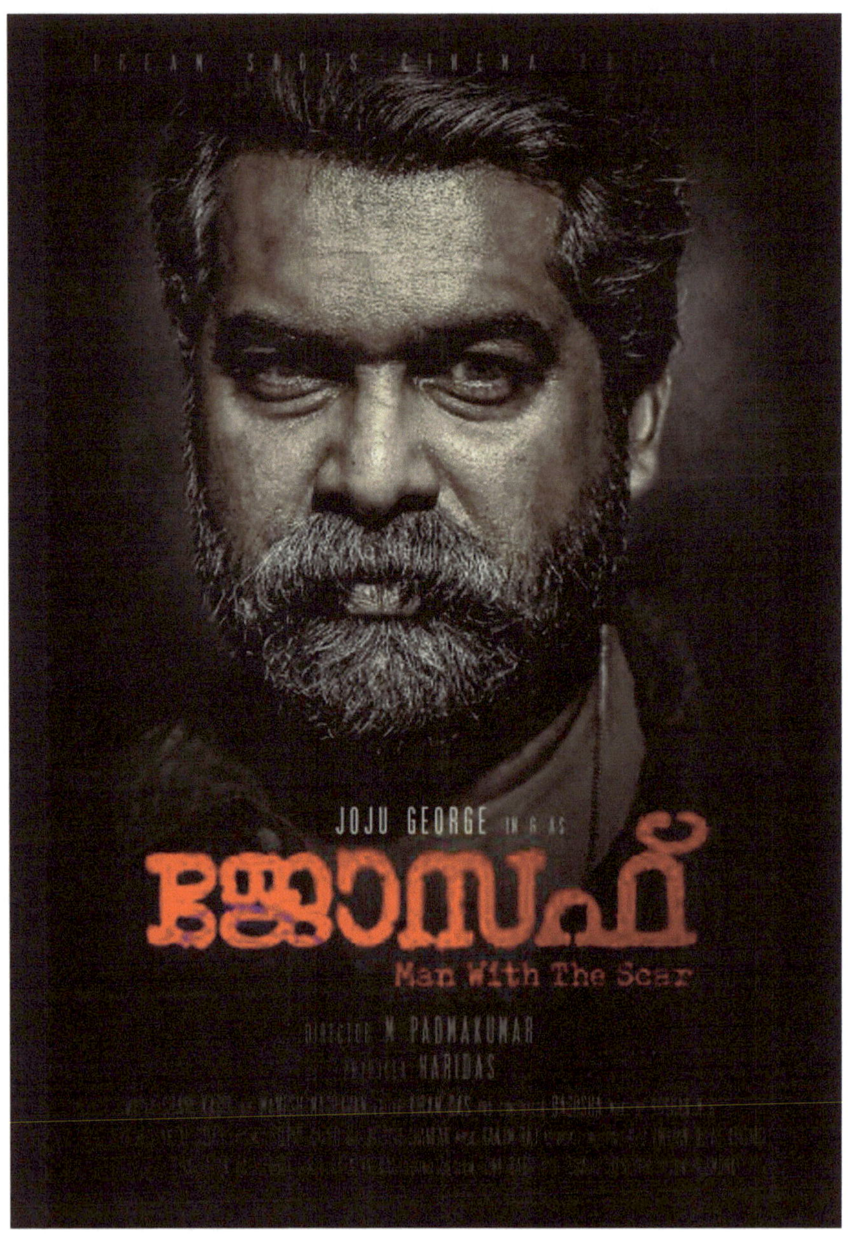

"You are free to paint any image that will impress you.
A living person needs to be asked permission to
draw him/her. However, I am a too big fan of
lalettan... So I draw lalettan"

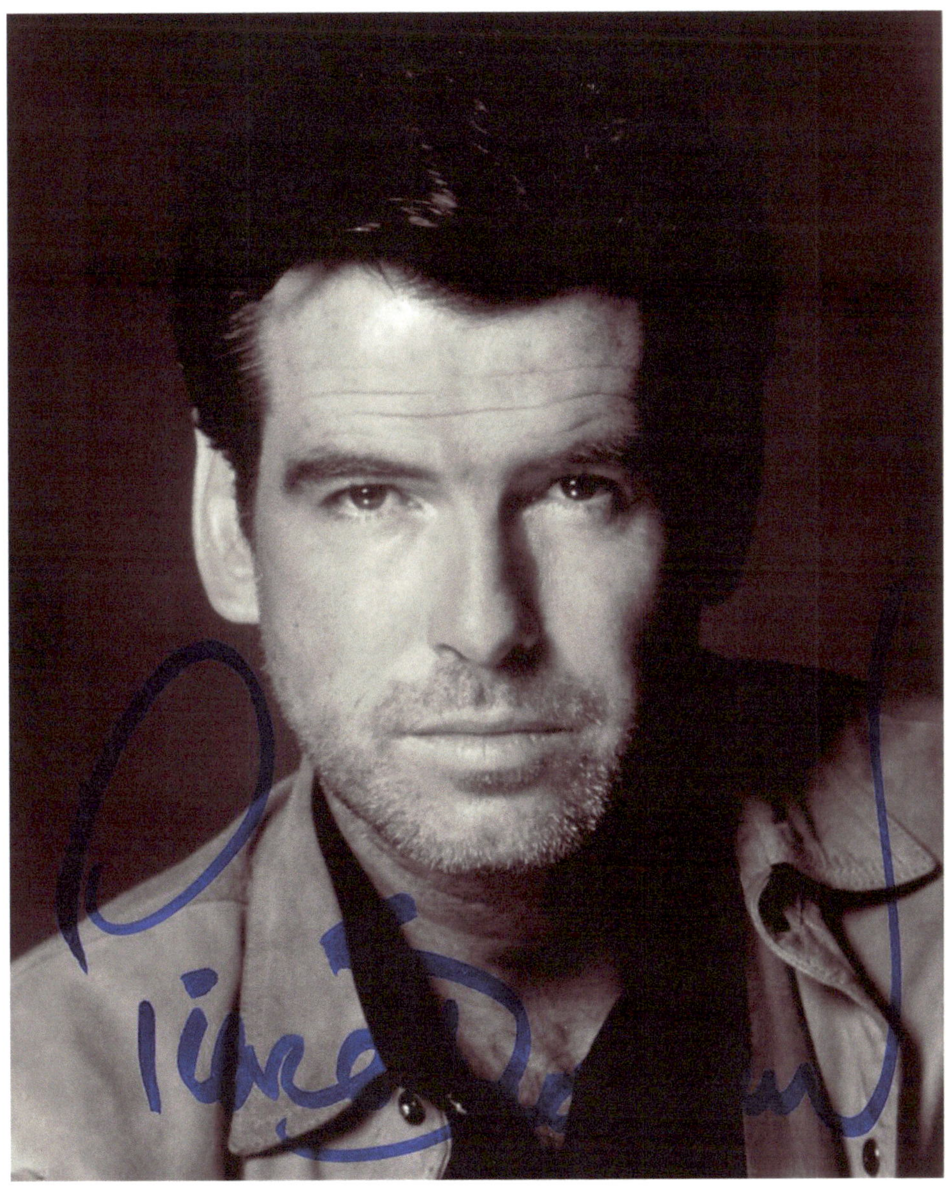

Sree Sankara
College in Memories

This is my first pencil drawing that I drew observing a person, which was done while sitting in the silence of the college library. The outsides of the library were often loud with demonstrations of college strikes and of political parties. I thank you for coming in and sitting for me in that silence. I didn't go to the library to get books. The picture must be drawn somehow. It's always quiet down there. No one is annoying either.

When I was the secretary of the arts club, I saw the talents of many people. But what are competitions for ? What do competitions give us ? It is better not to participate in it. Not everyone is a good judge. Many are incompetent. They are the judges of our creations and talents. Why should we compete to satisfy their stupidity and ignorance ? They chain our ideas then and there. This chain should be gone. In many venues, it is the parents who compete. They fight each other. For what ? Is it to nurture someone who has no idea ? You are the only one who knows your ideas and point of view.

"Freedom is being you without anyone's permission !"

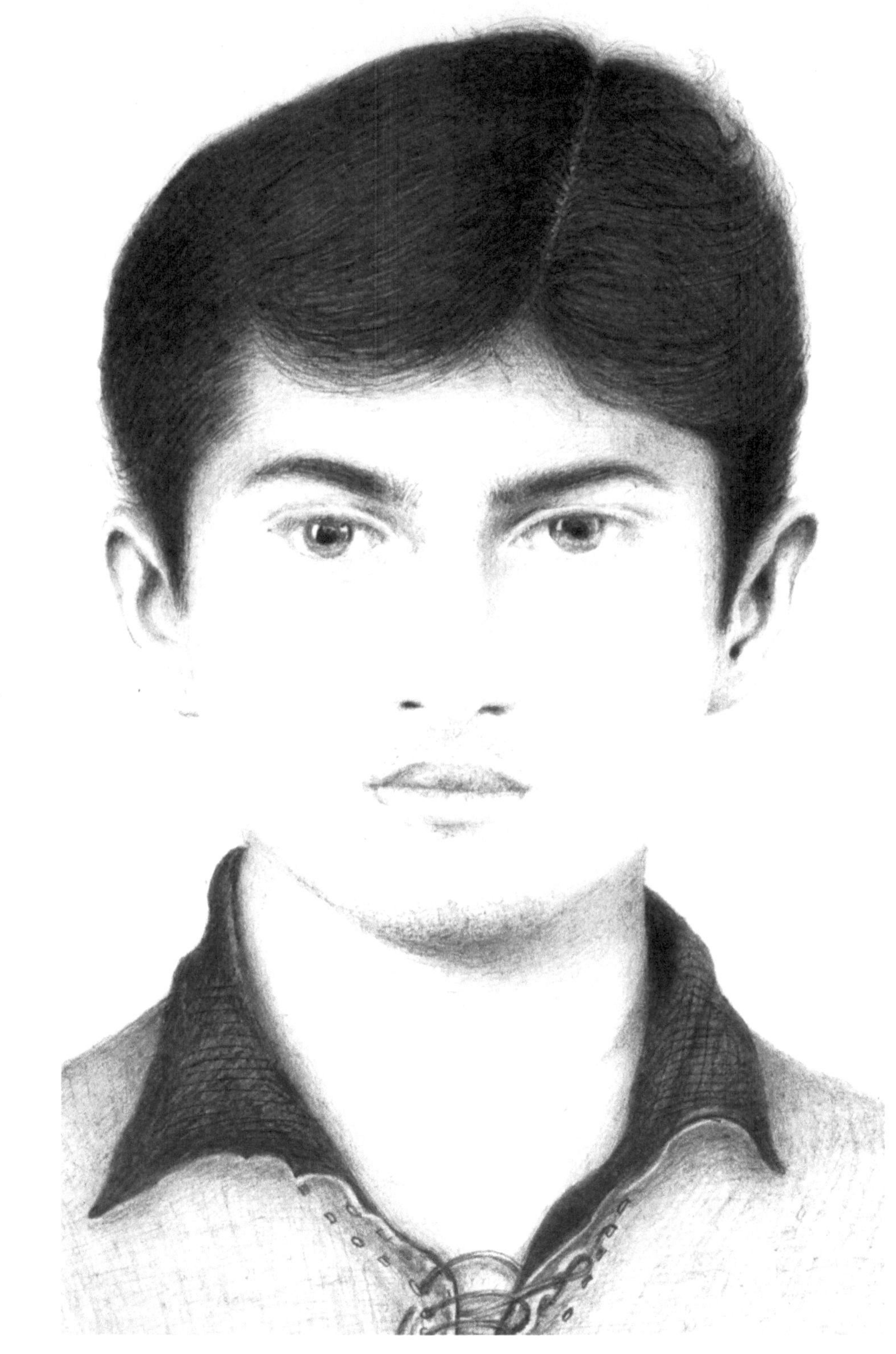

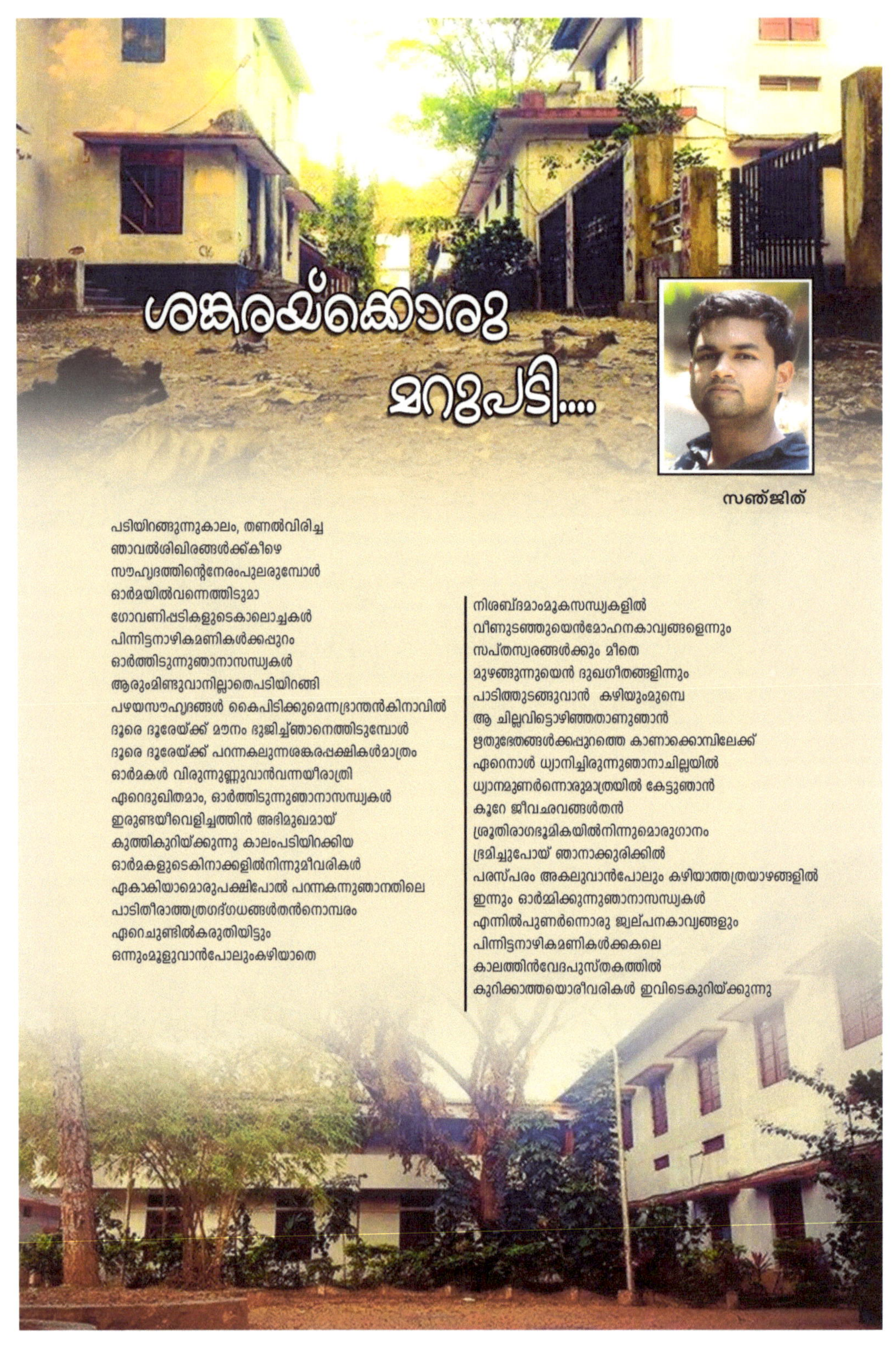

ശങ്കരയ്ക്കൊരു മറുപടി....

സഞ്ജിത്

പടിയിറങ്ങുന്നുകാലം, തണൽവിരിച്ച
ഞാവൽശിഖിരങ്ങൾക്കീഴെ
സൗഹൃദത്തിന്റെനേരംപുലരുമ്പോൾ
ഓർമയിൽവന്നെത്തിടുമാ
ഗോവണിപ്പടികളുടെകാലൊച്ചകൾ
പിന്നിട്ടനാഴികമണികൾക്കപ്പുറം
ഓർത്തിടുന്നുഞാനാസന്ധ്യകൾ
ആരുംമിണ്ടുവാനില്ലാതെപടിയിറങ്ങി
പഴയസൗഹൃദങ്ങൾ കൈപിടിക്കുമെന്നഭ്രാന്തൻകിനാവിൽ
ദൂരെ ദൂരേയ്ക്ക് മൗനം ഭുജിച്ച്ഞാനെത്തിടുമ്പോൾ
ദൂരെ ദൂരേയ്ക്ക് പറന്നകലുന്നശങ്കരപ്പക്ഷികൾമാത്രം
ഓർമകൾ വിരുന്നുണ്ണുവാൻവന്നയീരാത്രി
ഏറെദുഖിതമാം, ഓർത്തിടുന്നുഞാനാസന്ധ്യകൾ
ഇരുണ്ടയീവെളിച്ചത്തിൻ അഭിമുഖമായ്
കുത്തികുറിയ്ക്കുന്നു കാലംപടിയിറക്കിയ
ഓർമകളുടെകിനാക്കളിൽനിന്നുമീവരികൾ
ഏകാകിയായൊരുപക്ഷിപോൽ പറന്നകന്നുഞാനന്തിലെ
പാടിതീരാത്തത്രഗദ്ഗധങ്ങൾതൻനൊനാമ്പരം
ഏറെചുണ്ടിൽകരുതിയിട്ടും
ഒന്നുംമൂളുവാൻപോലുംകഴിയാതെ

നിശബ്ദമാംമൂകസന്ധ്യകളിൽ
വീണുടഞ്ഞുയെൻമോഹനകാവ്യങ്ങളെന്നും
സപ്തസ്വരങ്ങൾക്കും മീതെ
മുഴങ്ങുന്നുയെൻ ദുഖഗീതങ്ങളിന്നും
പാടിതുടങ്ങുവാൻ കഴിയുമുമ്പെ
ആ ചില്ലവിട്ടൊഴിഞ്ഞതാണുഞാൻ
ഋതുഭേദങ്ങൾക്കപ്പുറത്തെ കാണാക്കാമ്പിലേക്ക്
ഏനൊൾ ധ്യാനിച്ചിരുന്നുഞാനാചില്ലയിൽ
ധ്യാനമുണർന്നൊരുമാത്രയിൽ കേട്ടുഞാൻ
കൂറേ ജീവചരവങ്ങൾതൻ
ശ്രുതിരാഗഭൂമികയിൽനിന്നുമൊരുഗാനം
ഭ്രമിച്ചുപോയ് ഞാനാക്കുരിക്കിൽ
പരസ്പരം അകലുവാൻപോലും കഴിയാത്തത്രയാഴങ്ങളിൽ
ഇന്നും ഓർമ്മിക്കുന്നുഞാനാസന്ധ്യകൾ
എന്നിൽപുണർന്നൊരു ജ്വല്പനകാവ്യങ്ങളും
പിന്നിട്ടനാഴികമണികൾക്കകലെ
കാലത്തിൻവേദപുസ്തകത്തിൽ
കുറിക്കാത്തയൊരീവരികൾ ഇവിടെകുറിയ്ക്കുന്നു

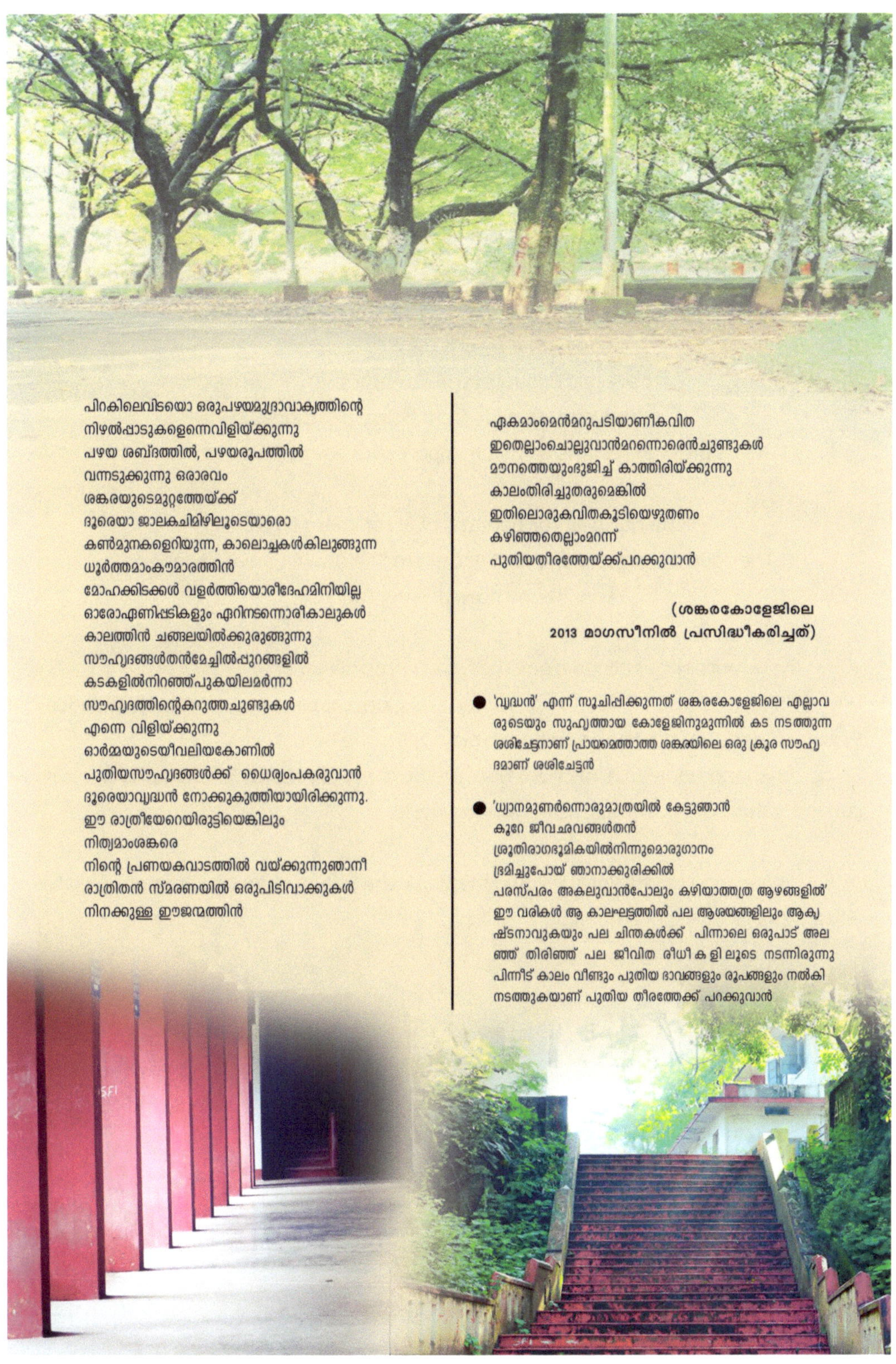

പിറകിലെവിടെയൊ ഒരുപഴയമുദ്രാവാക്യത്തിന്റെ
നിഴൽപ്പാടുകളെന്നെവിളിയ്ക്കുന്നു
പഴയ ശബ്ദത്തിൽ, പഴയരൂപത്തിൽ
വന്നടുക്കുന്നു ഒരരവം
ശങ്കരയുടെമുറ്റത്തേയ്ക്ക്
ദൂരെയാ ജാലകചിമിഴിലൂടെയാരൊ
കൺമുനകളെറിയുന്ന, കാലൊച്ചകൾകിലുങ്ങുന്ന
ധൂർത്തമാംകൗമാരത്തിൻ
മോഹക്കിടക്കൾ വളർത്തിയൊരീദേഹമിനിയില്ല
ഓരോഏണിപ്പടികളും ഏറിനടന്നൊരീകാലുകൾ
കാലത്തിൻ ചങ്ങലയിൽക്കുരുങ്ങുന്നു
സൗഹൃദങ്ങൾതൻമേച്ചിൽപ്പുറങ്ങളിൽ
കടകളിൽനിറഞ്ഞ്പുകയിലമർന്നാ
സൗഹൃദത്തിന്റെകറുത്തചുണ്ടുകൾ
എന്നെ വിളിയ്ക്കുന്നു
ഓർമ്മയുടെയീവലിയകോണിൽ
പുതിയസൗഹൃദങ്ങൾക്ക് ധൈര്യംപകരുവാൻ
ദൂരെയാവ്യദ്ധൻ നോക്കുകുത്തിയായിരിക്കുന്നു.
ഈ രാത്രീയേറെയിരുട്ടിയെങ്കിലും
നിത്യമാംശങ്കരെ
നിന്റെ പ്രണയകവാടത്തിൽ വയ്ക്കുന്നുഞാനീ
രാത്രിതൻ സ്മരണയിൽ ഒരുപിടിവാക്കുകൾ
നിനക്കുള്ള ഈജന്മത്തിൻ

ഏകമാംമെൻമറുപടിയാണീകവിത
ഇതെല്ലാംചൊല്ലുവാൻമറന്നൊരെൻചുണ്ടുകൾ
മൗനത്തെയുംഭുജിച്ച് കാത്തിരിയ്ക്കുന്നു
കാലംതിരിച്ചുതരുമെങ്കിൽ
ഇതിലൊരുകവിതകൂടിയെഴുതണം
കഴിഞ്ഞതെല്ലാംമറന്ന്
പുതിയതീരത്തേയ്ക്ക്പറക്കുവാൻ

(ശങ്കരകോളേജിലെ
2013 മാഗസീനിൽ പ്രസിദ്ധീകരിച്ചത്)

● 'വ്യദ്ധൻ' എന്ന് സൂചിപ്പിക്കുന്നത് ശങ്കരകോളേജിലെ എല്ലാവ
രുടെയും സുഹൃത്തായ കോളേജിനുമുന്നിൽ കട നടത്തുന്ന
ശശിചേട്ടനാണ് പ്രായമെത്താത്ത ശങ്കരയിലെ ഒരു ക്രൂര സൗഹൃ
ദമാണ് ശശിചേട്ടൻ

● 'ധ്യാനമുണർന്നൊരുമാത്രയിൽ കേട്ടുഞാൻ
കൂറേ ജീവചരവങ്ങൾതൻ
ശ്രുതിരാഗഭൂമികയിൽനിന്നുമൊരുഗാനം
ഭ്രമിച്ചുപോയ് ഞാനാക്കുരിക്കിൽ
പരസ്പരം അകലുവാൻപോലും കഴിയാത്തത്ര ആഴങ്ങളിൽ'
ഈ വരികൾ ആ കാലഘട്ടത്തിൽ പല ആശയങ്ങളിലും ആകൃ
ഷ്ടനാവുകയും പല ചിന്തകൾക്ക് പിന്നാലെ ഒരുപാട് അല
ഞ്ഞ് തിരിഞ്ഞ് പല ജീവിത രീധീകളിലൂടെ നടന്നിരുന്നു
പിന്നീട് കാലം വീണ്ടും പുതിയ ഭാവങ്ങളും രൂപങ്ങളും നൽകി
നടത്തുകയാണ് പുതിയ തീരത്തേക്ക് പറക്കുവാൻ

Strive to Succeed

It's been a long time since I've had to stay away from amidst the colors. But I have to start drawing some time now. I'm going to play football these days. It gives me some happiness for a while. So, football has become something that I can't stop now.

I will play to win. But I lose some games by a good margin. However, playing football is an experience that never fails me.

"I do what I feel is right...
I have had unsuccessful attempts.
But I learned a lot from those paintings.
I give my failures as much importance as my success..."

Do not play for defeats; play for them to win.
The football game is the joy I got when the drawing was stopped.
I am happy now, playing football.

Now football has become one that I can't stop playing.
"Sports doesn't question anybody's religion, caste, creed, and bank balance. Everybody is equal, but the one who can play well is the hero!"
Cristiano Ronaldo is my hero because he is my favourite football player. He is currently the most charitable athlete in the world.

"When you have talent, if you don't work the talent, then you are not going to win anything." - Cristiano Ronaldo

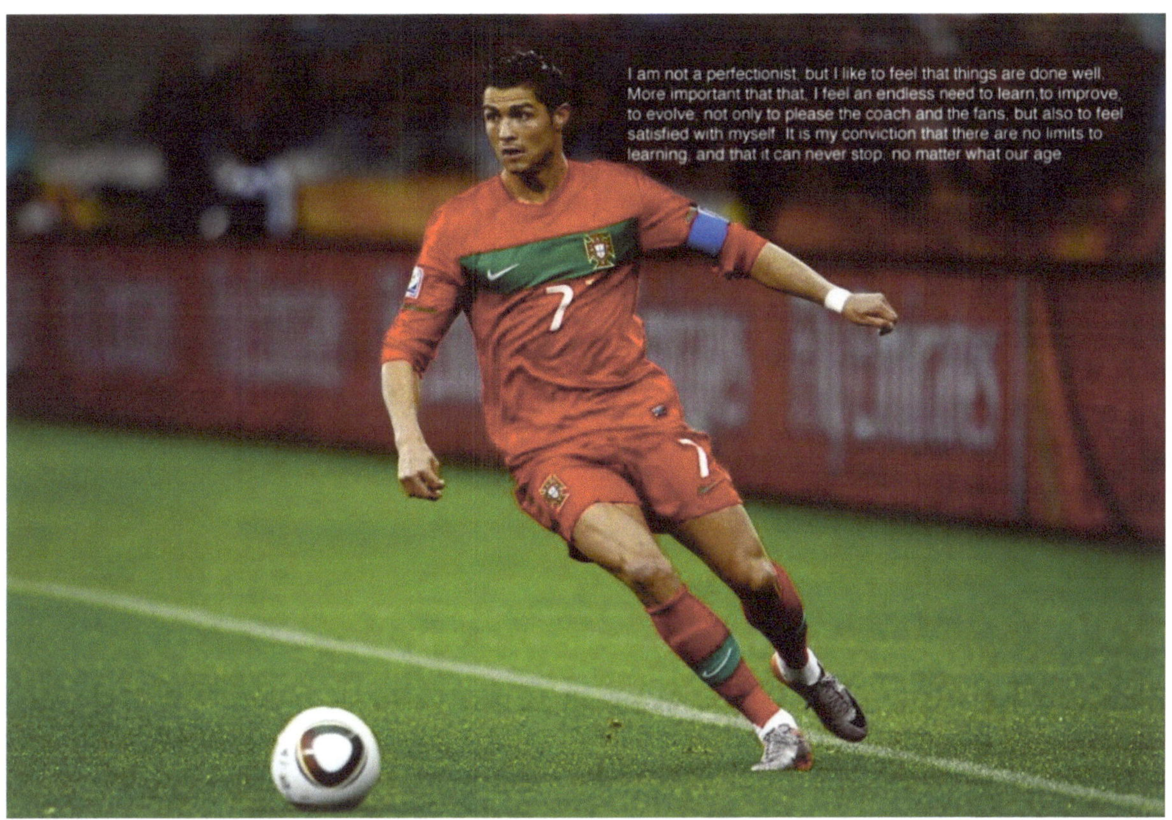

"I am not a perfectionist, but I like to feel things are done well. More important than that. I feel an endless need to learn, to improve, and to evolve, not only to please the coach and the fans but also to feel satisfied with myself. It is my conviction that there are no limits to learning, and that it can never stop, no matter our age."

If you are a scrutinizer,
you will find it !

A picture that impressed me... I got to enjoy their work while strolling through the university. It was also an exhibition in which everyone drew very well. I observe every picture. The knowledge gained from them is great. Even if it's just the drawing of a small line, I love every bit of knowledge I can get from it. While looking at all the pictures, one picture in particular stood out. It made me think for some seconds and a some more minutes for me to understand what they were trying to show with that picture. The picture passed through my eyes from very close. I only saw straight lines. Then I slowly focused my mind. I stepped back a little and observed the drawing. It was then that they realized what they had hidden in those straight lines. Every little shade goes into the black and shows off the black with a beautiful... white streak. I was angry with them. Because there was no creator present to explain that picture. The success of any picture is when the artiste explains it by staying alongside the picture. They are the only ones who can do it.

I have not been able to see many of books of art. If he had kept my distance from that picture, I would have understood that picture quicker. I loved the time and distance that took me to realise that I could understand the incomprehensible picture from afar but not closer and also loved the creation that they hid inside it. "Observing this picture from up close attracted the mind's ability to discover!"

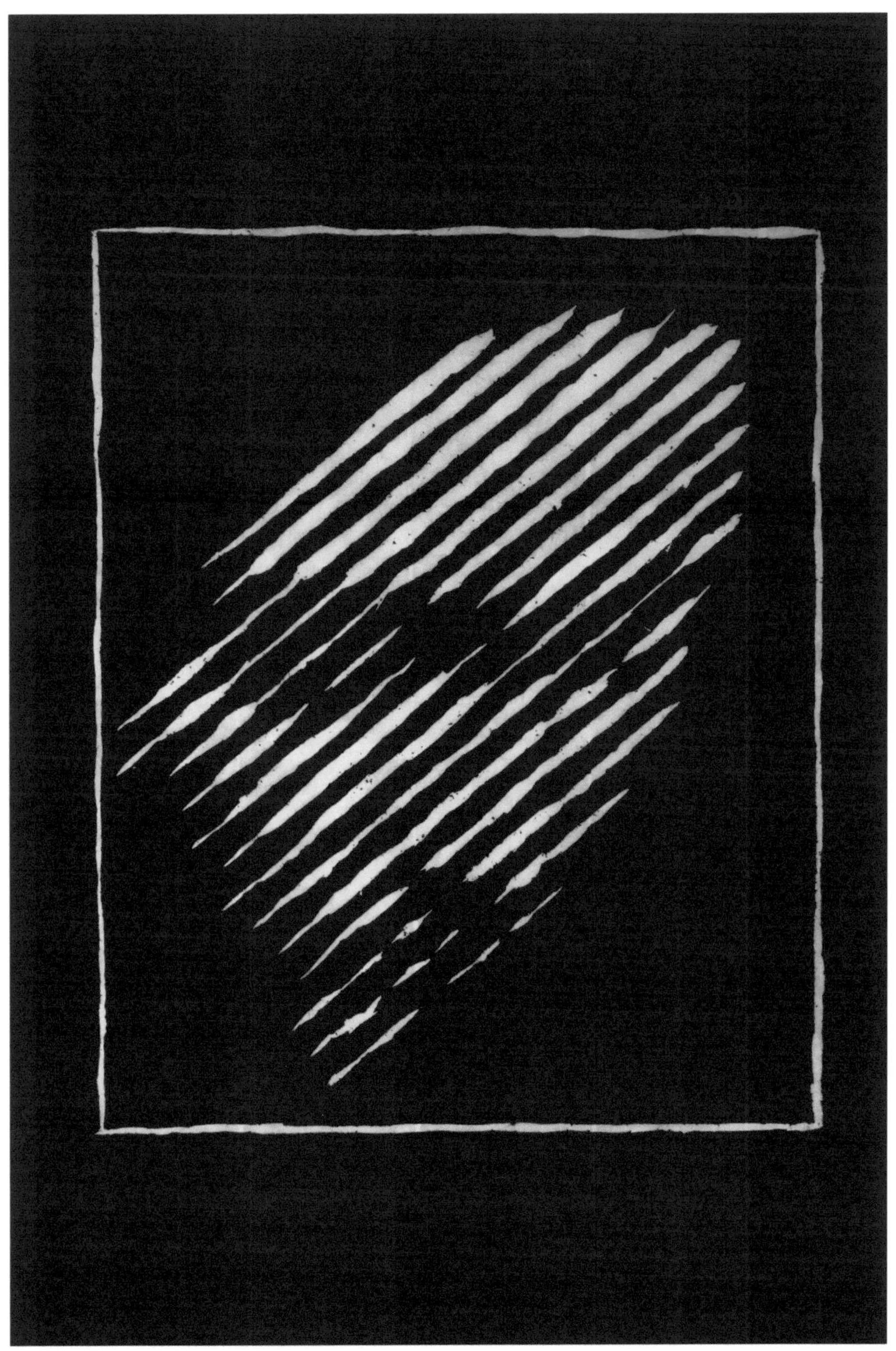

Do you belive that
India is a secular state..?

"Is India still a secular state?" Is secularism going to survive in India?

Do you believe that India is a secular state...?

I don't believe it. This is the latest news we came to know. But none of us would have thought about the term "secular state." We all owe an account on social media sites like Facebook, WhatsApp, Twitter, and so on. Everyone likes to share their own ideas. If we search for the word "secularism," we will love the meaning for sure.

If we happen to see secularism being violated somewhere, it is our turn to fight against it and save the real meaning of secularism.

"Always, we are ashamed of your death."

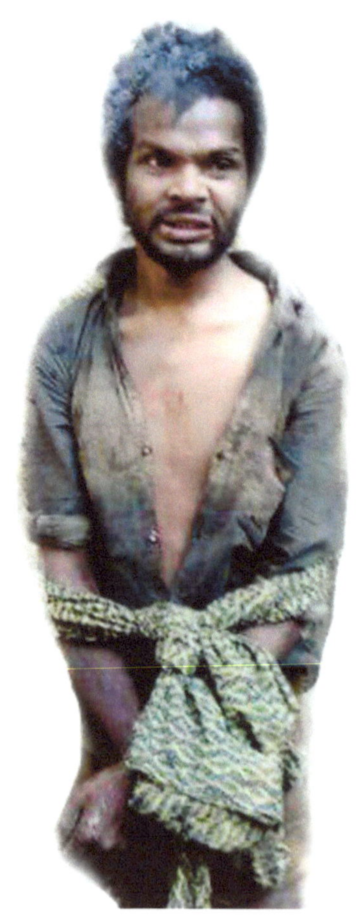

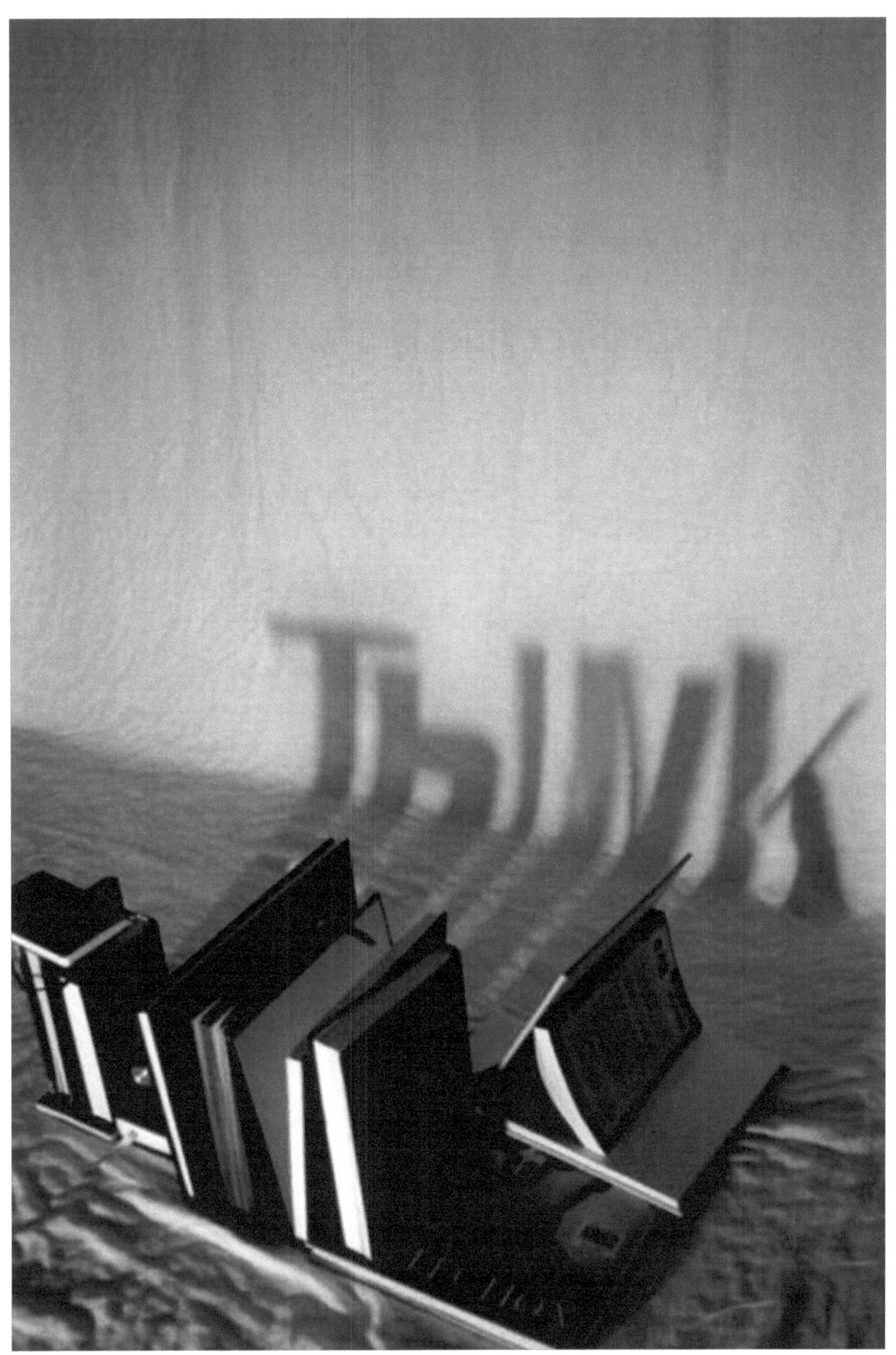

MY VOICE
MY WORDS

I live in my past, so I can't forget it.
I live in my memories, and I can't forget it.

Do not let my judgement be yours.

There was a time when there was a
pencil worth only one rupee.
Often, the pencil slipped from my hand,
breaking its tip, which also broke my heart.

Everyone thinks that the artist is an alcoholic;
this is the certificate of community.
However, I did not take that certificate.

I don't paint a picture with alcohol...
I am not drawing with alcohol. I do not need
alcohol to think. Occasionally, I use alcohol.
Alcohol gives comfort from some difficulties.

"Even so, don't submit your life to alcohol."

THEY SEE MY
DISABILITY,
I SEE MY
ABILITY.

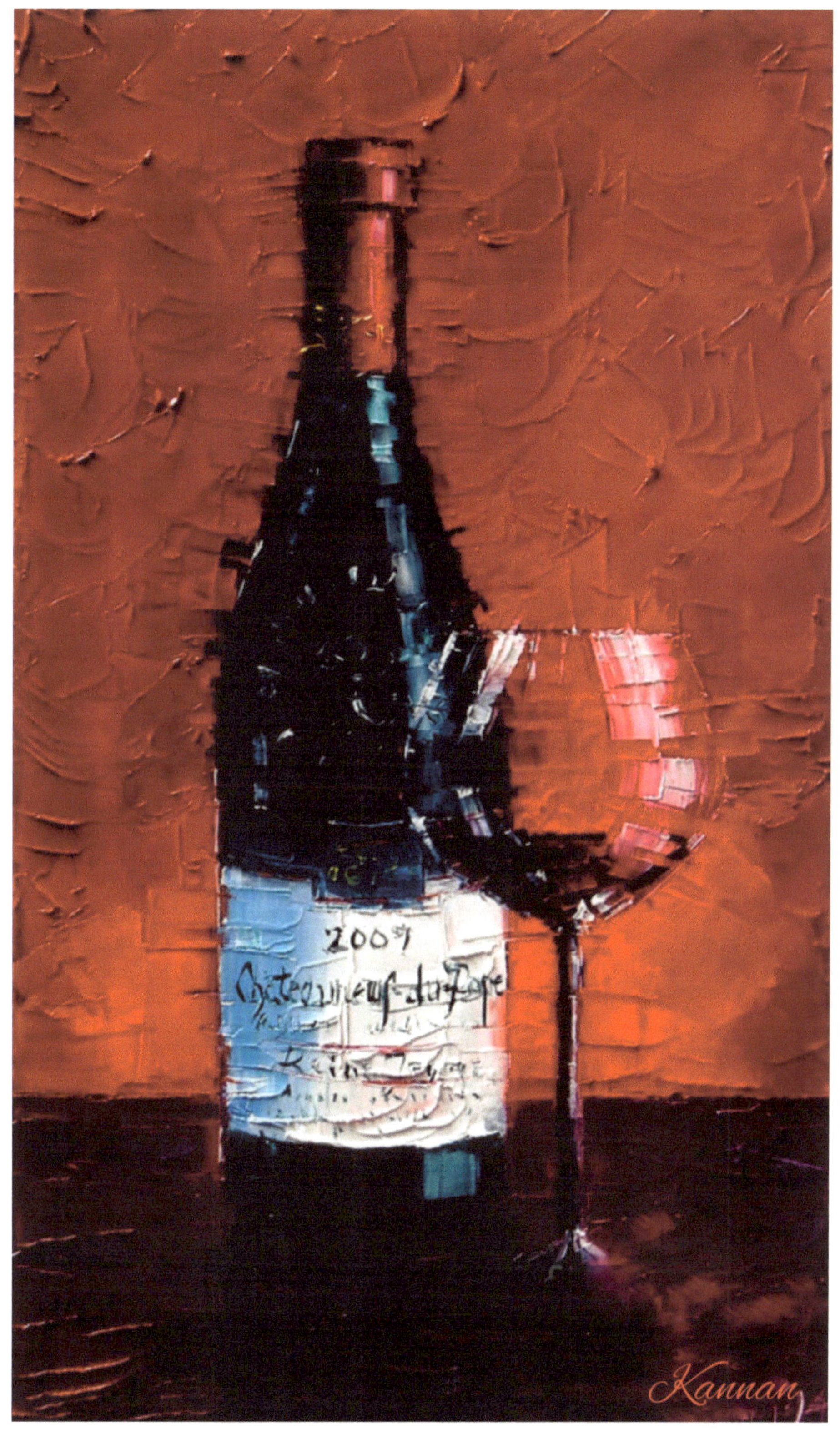

2009
Châteauneuf-du-Pape
Kannan

The Deep Sea

Sometimes 'eyes' attract me mysteriously. And then, I think about the depth of the sea because I like it. I can't explain the beauty of those eyes. The eyes are not conscious of their beauty.
Girls always think that if a person watches them, they believe that the person is rude or nasty. We cannot blame them because staring is a common phenomenon.
I always love to watch the depth of those eyes, and then, how can I explain to them that their eyes are very attractive...? If I do so, they won't believe me and won't understand my feelings for those eyes.

"There is a frontier between you and me.".

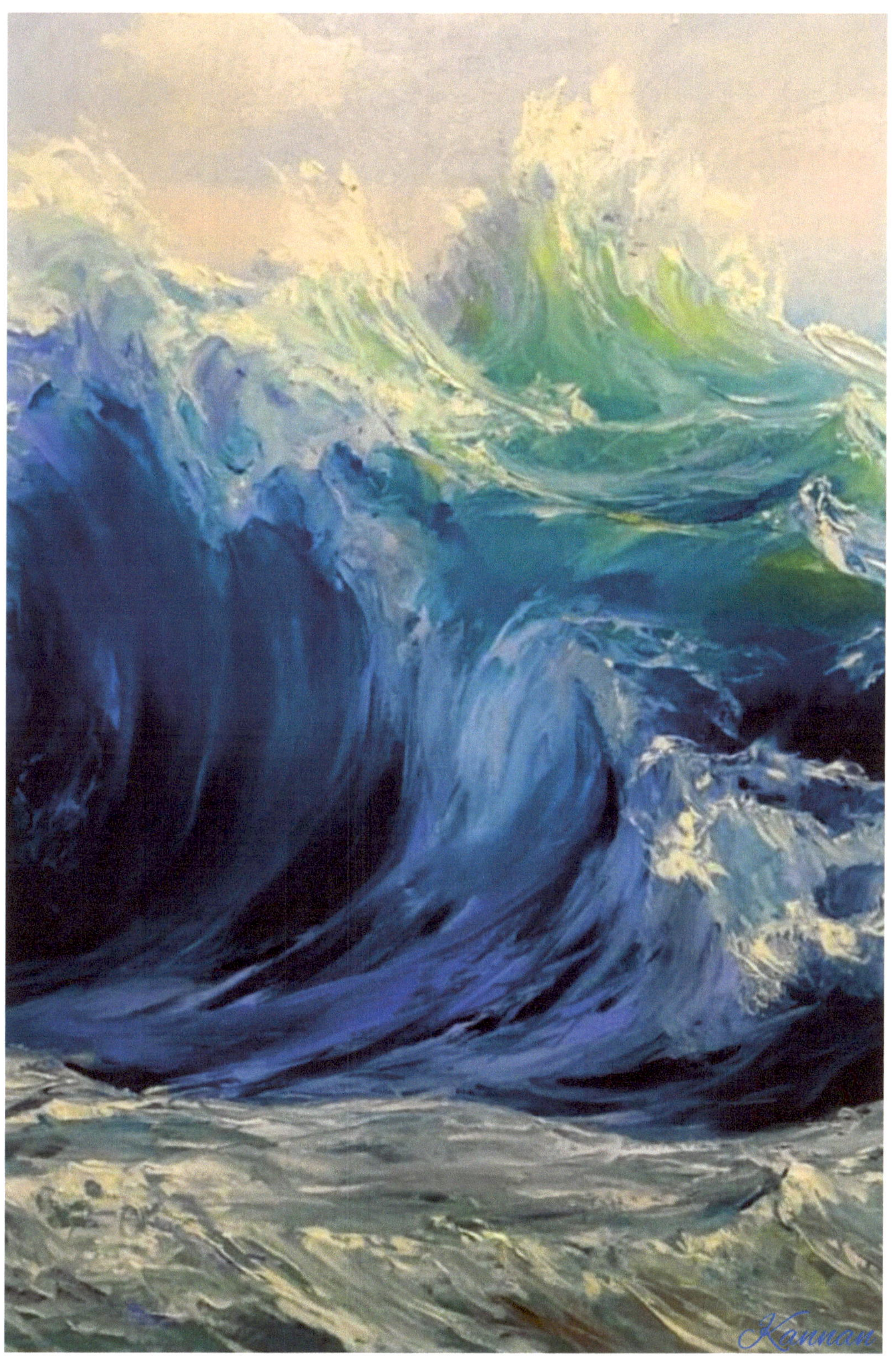

Simple Thoughts
of a Simple Heart

"Advanced mathematical problems are difficult to understand, but to someone who understands mathematics, a problem is simple."

The advanced-level mathematics problems are difficult to understand. However, for those who are aware of the principles, the lessons are simple. The same is true of paintings.

Topics like 'differentiation' and 'integration' have terrified me. This has prompted me to communicate through simple things. I draw pictures that are easy to understand.

I hope my paintings communicate easily. I do not use abstract codes to make the paintings. difficult to understand. Once I loved big thoughts, but not now...

The past has never come back, but I live on with the hope that I will get it back because I hate my present.

Some questions, like shadows, hunt me... These questions will continue to hunt me until I reach my world. It is time for me to yield to that hunt.

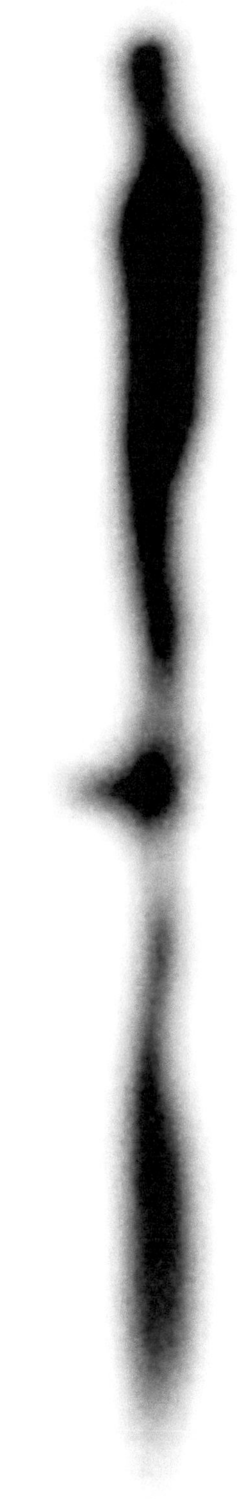

Deep in the Eyes

"Trying to go descend into the depths of the eyes is the same as traveling through the depths of an ocean. At times I wonder if eyes were the doors to the sea. But I can only think, right? Often, I try to draw the depths of the eyes, but it all ends up with a hard feeling such that it is impossible to draw. It is impossible to express that situation... Depending on the amount of melanin in the body, the color of the pupils also varies. For some, the beauty of the eyes is a plus point because of the melanin and their positive energy which is reflected in their eyes as a whole; the shape of the eye and the sparkle that can be emitted from it is a rare blessing that only a few people possess!"

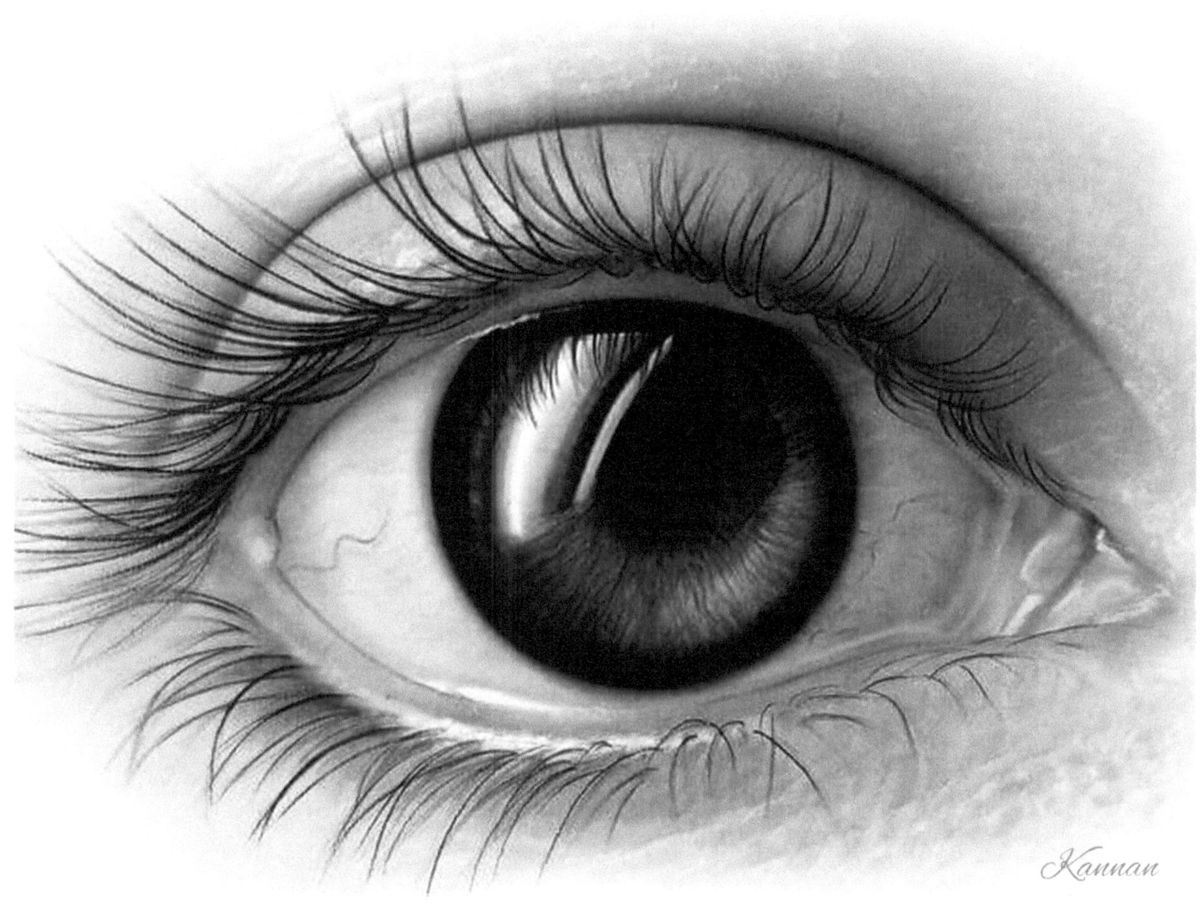

Kannan

LIFE

If there is one thing that I have learned in life, it is that the little things are the big things. Those tiny, daily deposits into the love account will give you far more happiness than any amount of money in your bank account.

You will soon see that your life would not be as rich and colourful without the mistakes of your past. So be gentler with yourself and see life for what it really is: a path of self-discovery, personal growth, and lifelong learning.

You change your life the second you make a decision from the depths of your heart to be a better, more dedicated human being. What takes months and years are the efforts you must apply to maintain that decision. And the best life-changing decision you will ever make is to live every moment of your days to the fullest.

"Nothing is perfect... Nothing is meant to be perfect. One's life is never supposed to be perfect, so you have to take the moments and make it perfect...."

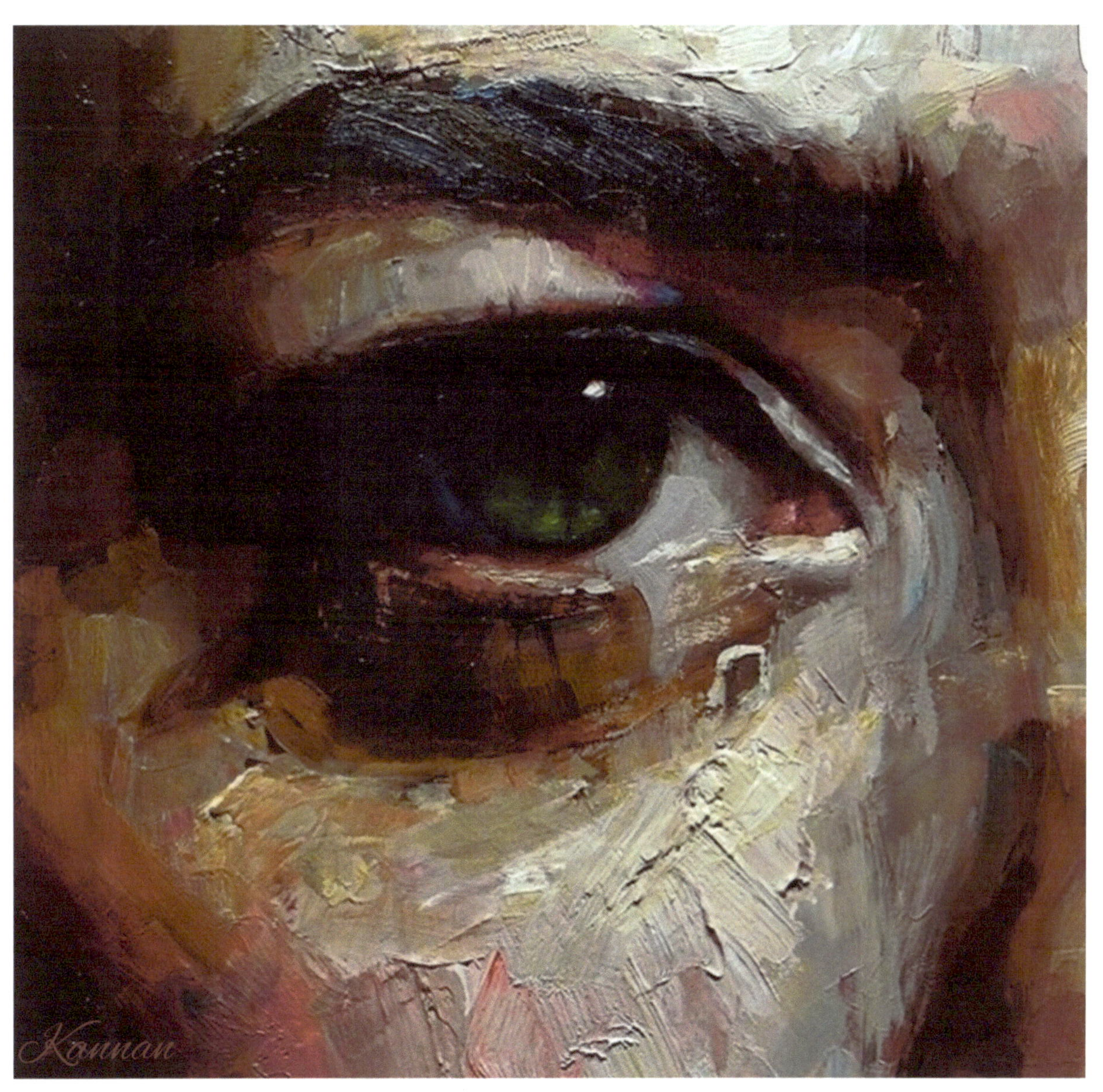
Konnan

Understanding Article 19(1)(a): The Freedom of Speech and Expression in India
Freedom of Speech and Expression (Article 19(1) (a)):

This freedom allows every citizen to express their thoughts and ideas through any communicable medium. It includes the right to voice one's opinion, to publish their ideas in print or online, and to broadcast them on radio, television, or any digital platform. However, this freedom is not absolute and is subject to reasonable restrictions on grounds of sovereignty and integrity of India, security of the state, friendly relations with foreign states, public order, decency, morality, or in relation to contempt of court, defamation, or incitement to an offence.

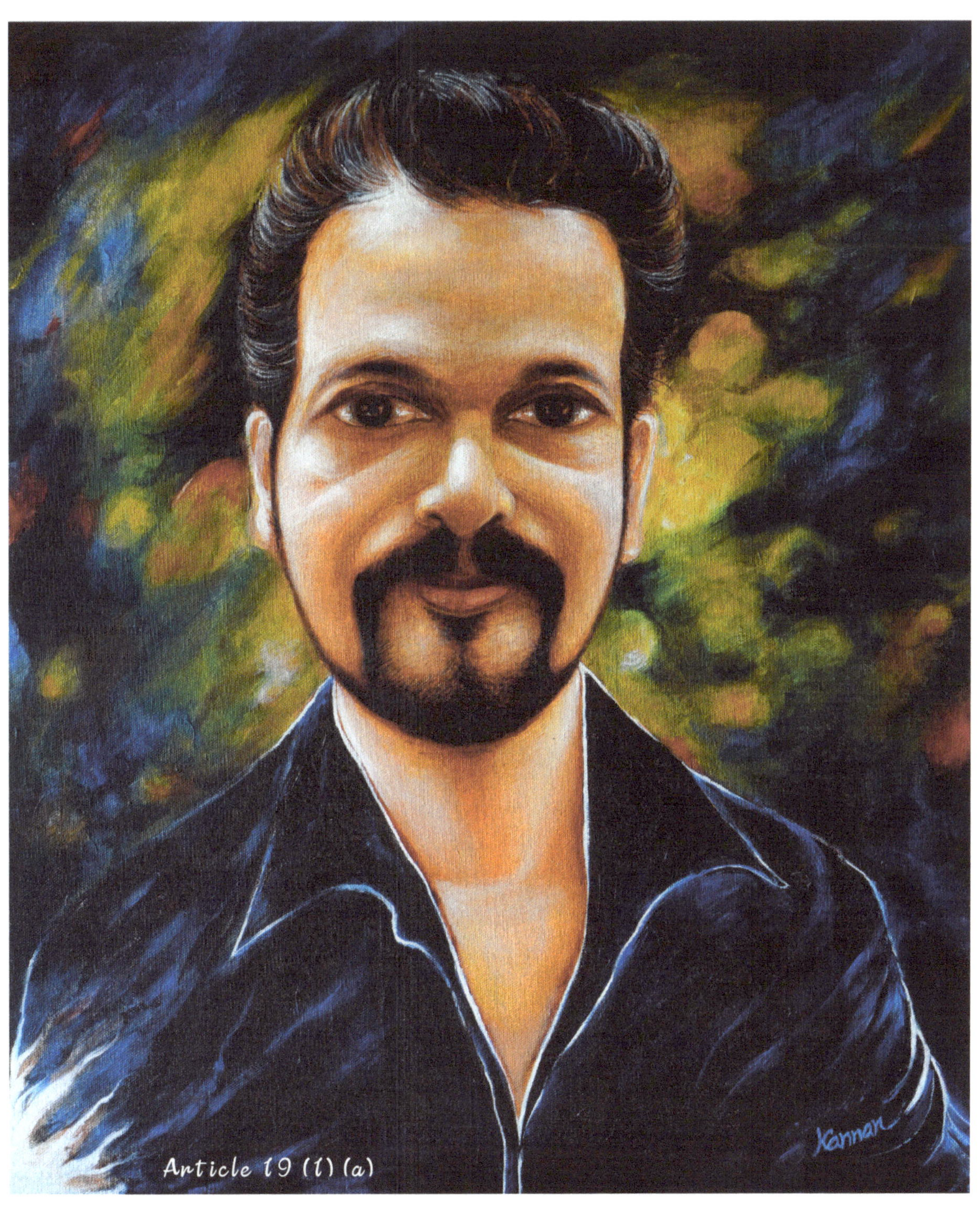

Sorry Father,
I could not grow up the way you wished.

Because of you,

I paint my dreams

Forever, my paintings are always

filled with your lovely colour

drops.

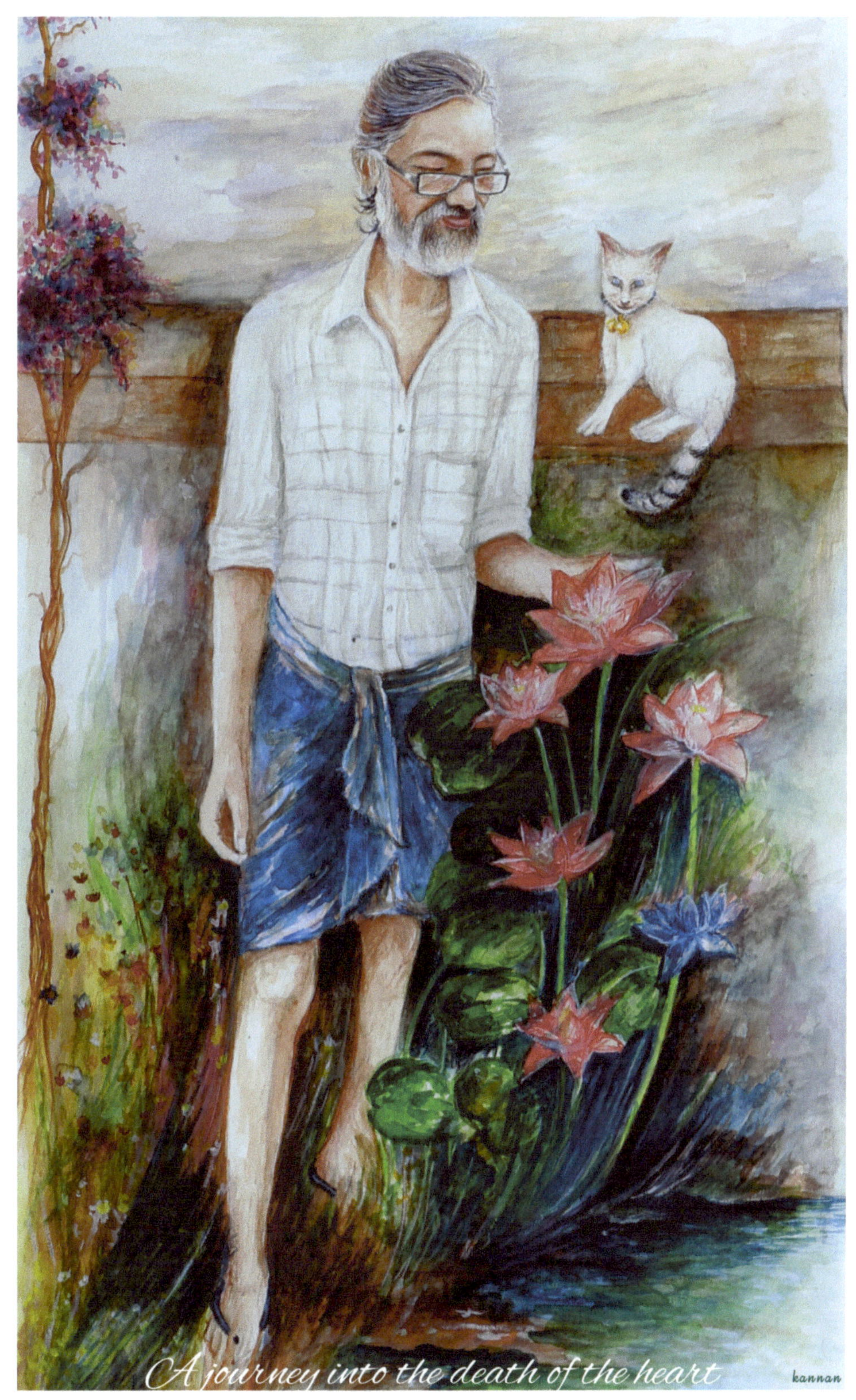

A journey into the death of the heart
kannan

The love shore of hopes.

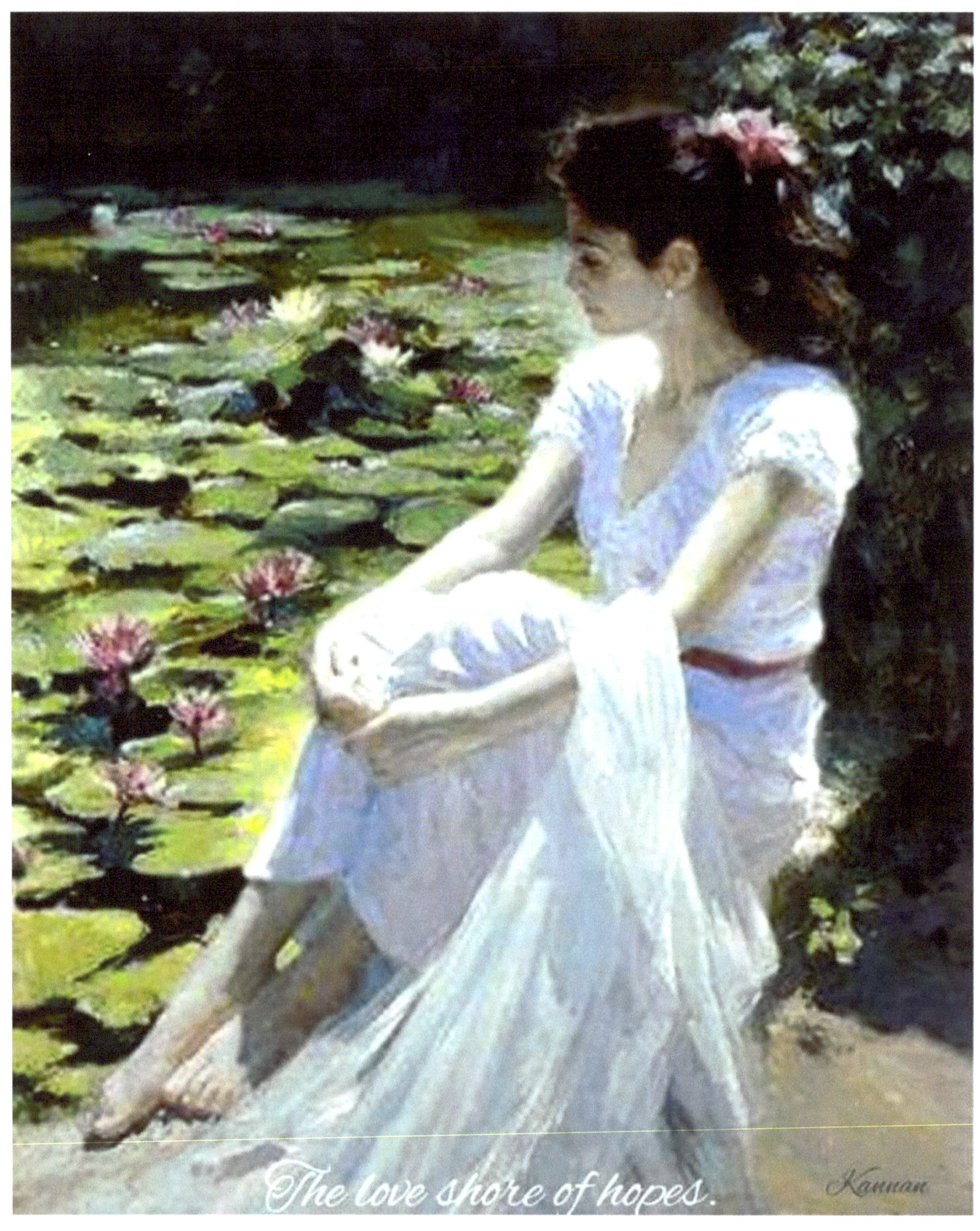

Blossom with love

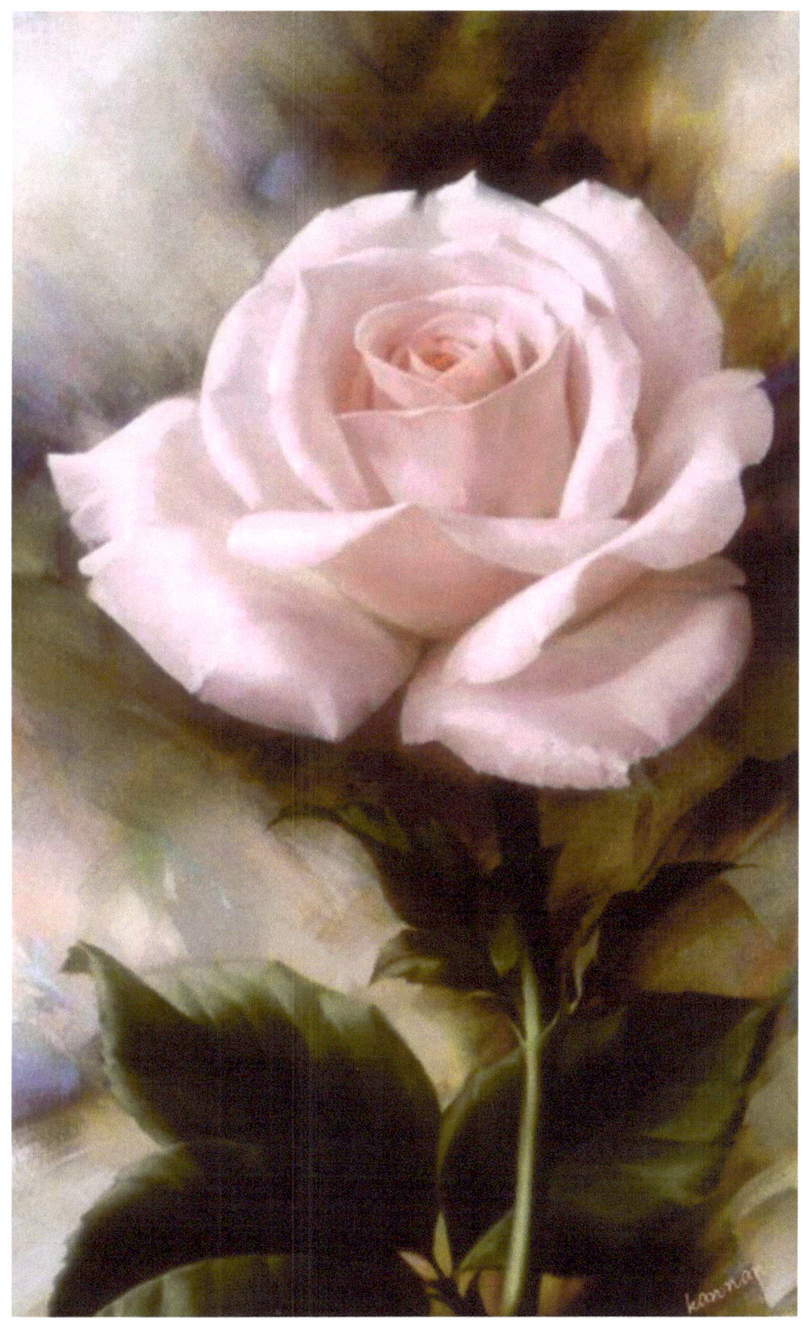

Angel of Flowers

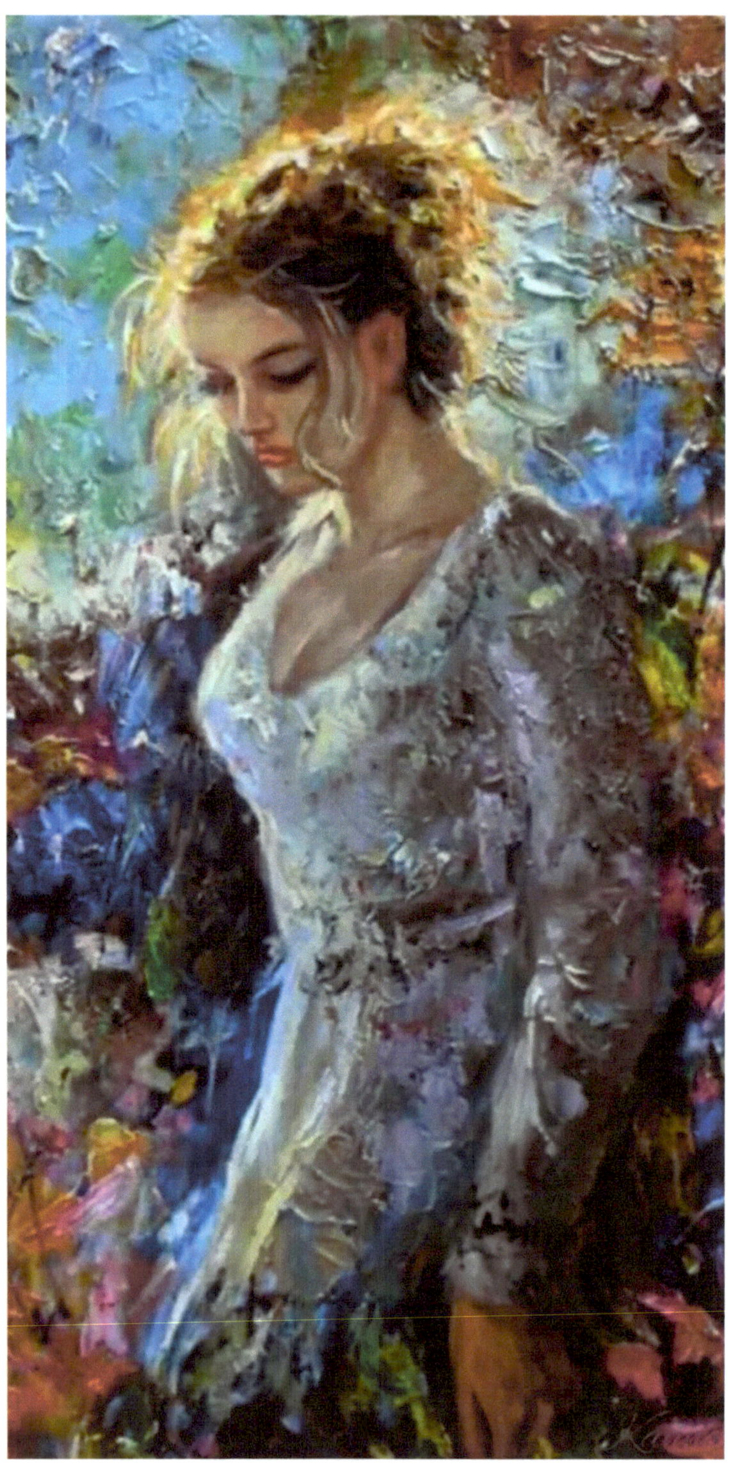

Flowers Don't Tell;
They Show.

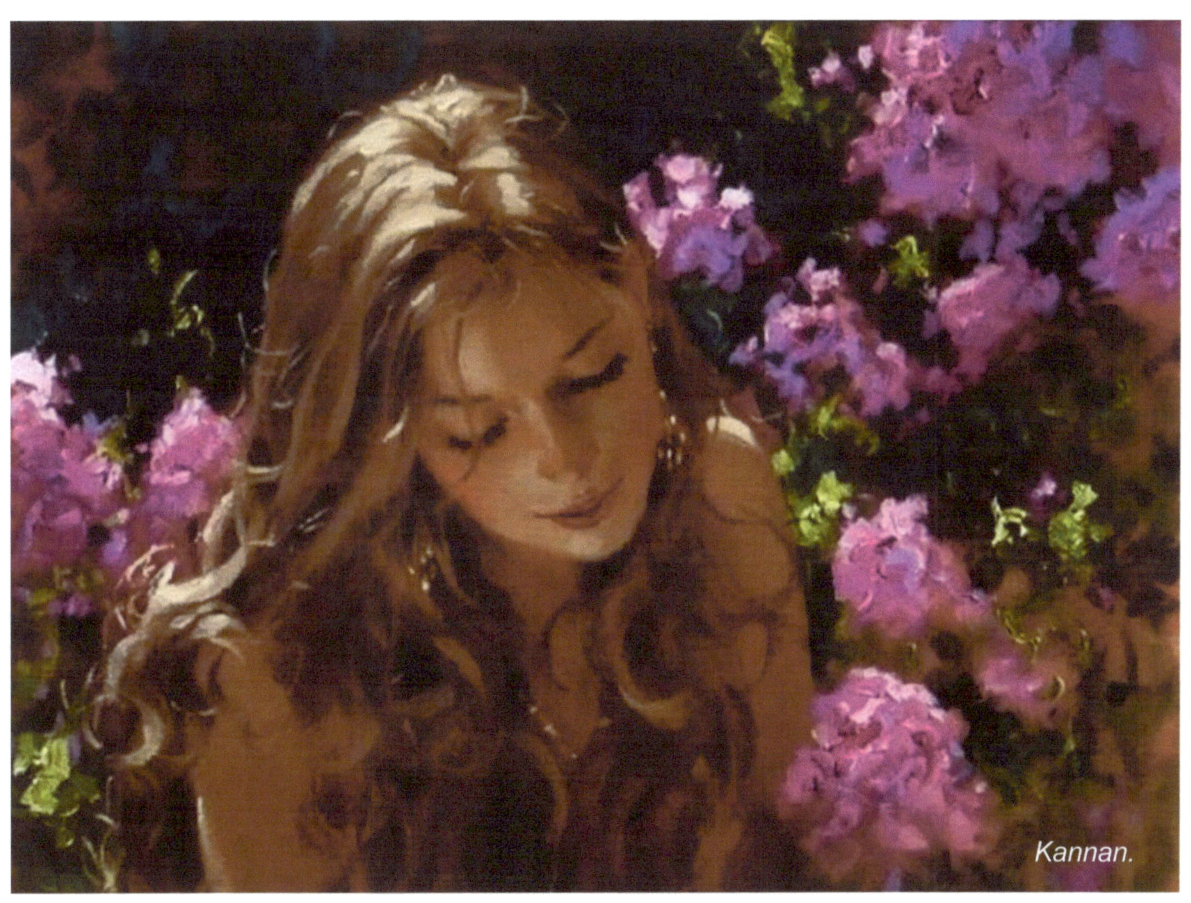

MY REQUEST IS FOR ALL THE PARENTS

Parents should not force their unfulfilled dreams on their children.
You never know what kind of talent he or she has or what they can
give to the country.
"A horse wearing blinders is able to know a single way
the horse runs only along the way
you are commanded".

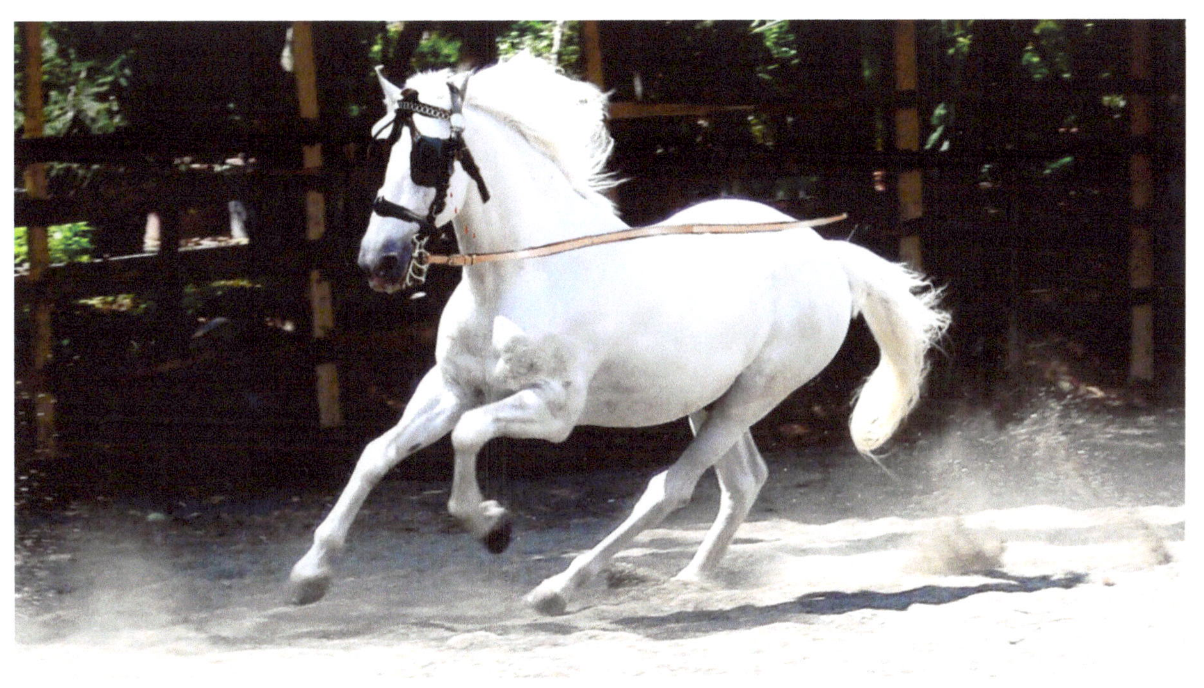

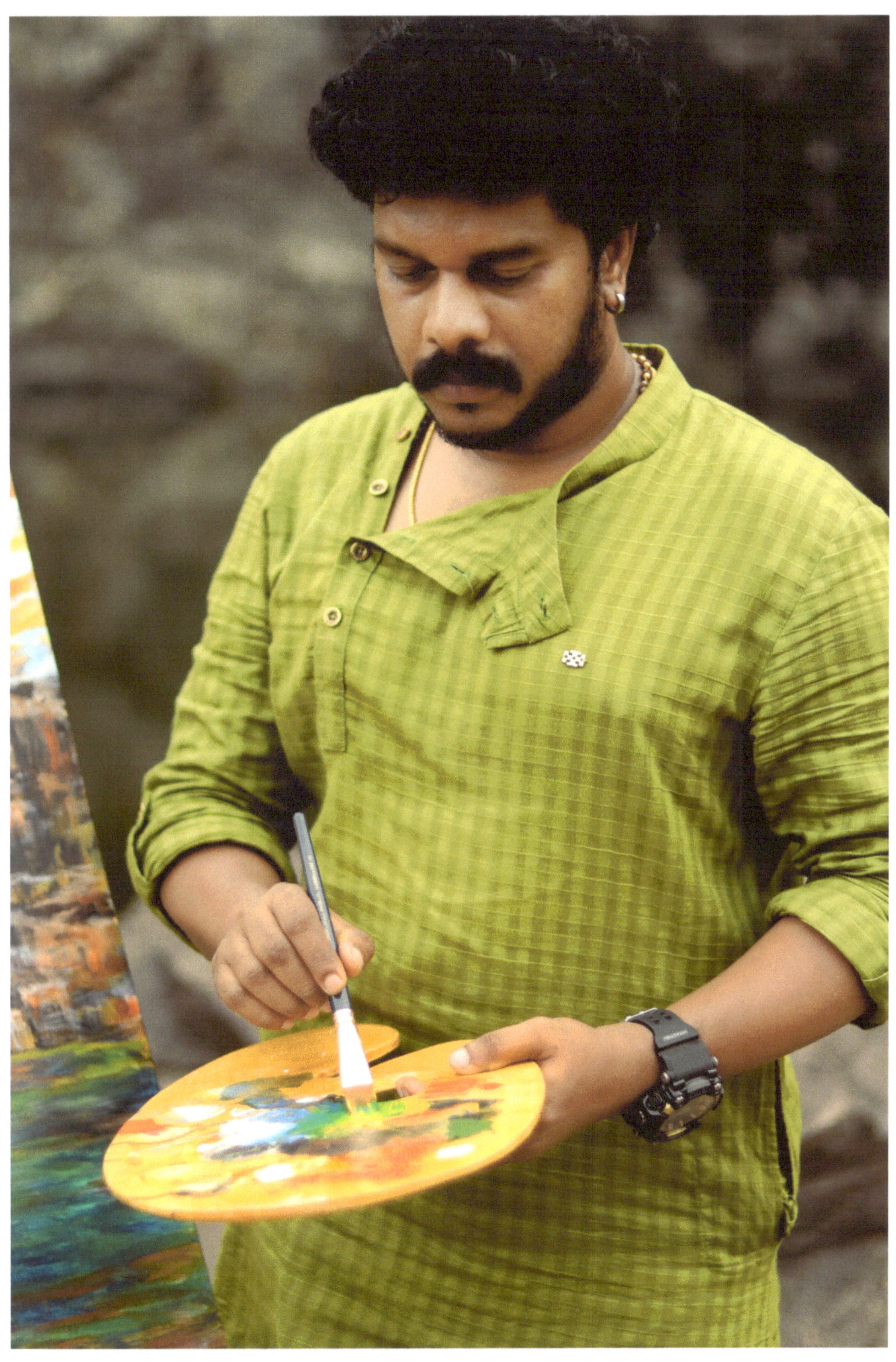

www.ingramcontent.com/pod-product-compliance
Lightning Source LLC
Chambersburg PA
CBHW041643110726
48005CB00003B/692